"*Talk Lean* is po regain control of
your agenda, bec(e greater impact
in your business, i methods shared
by Alan Palmer in you will prepare
for and engage in ...most importantly, the ways in
which you establish and manage key relationships in business and life
in general."
Tony Latham, Vice-President Finance, Unilever, North Asia

"Busy people do not have the time to misunderstand or be misunderstood,
and building confidence and trust early pays dividends. This book
identifies the traps we all fall into in dealing with others and provides
unique insight in how to be more productive, open and straightforward,
and hopefully feel better about the way we deal with our fellow citizens."
**Andrew Shilston, Non-Executive Director, BP; Non-Executive
Director, Circle Holdings; Chairman, Morgan Advanced Materials**

"Bored with long-winded, aimless meetings? Nervous about that difficult
conversation with your boss which you've been putting off? Alan Palmer's
clear and entertaining exposition of the brilliantly effective 'Interactifs'
training approach will transform how you deal with your colleagues,
clients and friends. Thoroughly recommended."
**Antonio E. Weiss, bestselling author of *Key Business Solutions* and
*101 Business Ideas That Will Change the Way You Work***

"Communicating clearly, effectively and directly is essential to our
professional and personal lives. Yet most of us are very poor at it,
particularly when faced with difficult or awkward situations. Alan Palmer's
refreshingly pragmatic and entertaining book shows us how to handle all
these situations and talk to people the way they like to be spoken to:
directly, to the point and with courtesy. This helps build trust and
confidence in our relationships. It is full of practical examples and captures
the essence of the highly successful 'Interactifs' training which I have
found invaluable."
**Flemming Morgan, President, Danone Medical Nutrition Division;
Member of Danone Executive Committee; Non-Executive Director,
Agrolimen**

"Even a small improvement in your communication skills can be life-changing. It only needs one or two people, in key situations, to say yes where they might have said no for the course of events to be radically altered. Just imagine if Chamberlain had been able to convince Hitler to come to Wimbledon rather than to invade Poland; or if Louis XVI had persuaded Danton to stay for dinner. *Talk Lean* will help you make major improvements in your communications skills. It shows you how you can systematically give yourself the best chance of achieving the outcome you want from meetings and conversations, swiftly and without upsetting the relationship."
Hugh Easterbrook, Managing Partner, Flying Buttress Partners Ltd

"I LOVED this book. At a time when everyone, and especially busy executives, have to make the best use of every minute in their overextended lives, here is a book that is really helpful. Alan Palmer's book is brimming with excellent insights and practical solutions to working more effectively with your colleagues, collaborating with your Board members and having more fun with your friends and family. This book delivers a message that needs to be heard and acted upon by many people in the business world and delivers it in an amusing and compelling manner."
Vivien Godfrey, CEO, US National Milk Processors' Organization (Milk Mustache)

"A clear and concise handbook for communicating efficiently and effectively with all types of people. It will help you to close the all-important but often narrow gap between success and failure in meetings."
Ridgely Cinquegrana, President, Neptune Capital; President, United Perfumes; former President, Loewe LVMH

TALK LEAN

Shorter Meetings.
Quicker Results. Better Relations.

Alan H. Palmer

On the basis of original ideas and a framework
("The Interactifs Discipline") conceived and developed by
Philippe de Lapoyade

With contributions from Clément Toulemonde

CAPSTONE
A Wiley Brand

This edition first published 2014
© 2014 Alan H. Palmer

The Interactifs Discipline® is an original teaching approach developed by Philippe de Lapoyade and protected under copyright law. The Interactifs company is the owner of the relevant intellectual property rights and enjoys exclusive rights to the exploitation of the Interactifs Discipline.

Registered office

John Wiley & Sons Ltd, The Atrium, Southern Gate, Chichester, West Sussex, PO19 8SQ, UK

For details of our global editorial offices, for customer services and for information about how to apply for permission to reuse the copyright material in this book please see our website at www.wiley.com.

The right of the author to be identified as the author of this work has been asserted in accordance with the Copyright, Designs and Patents Act 1988.

Wiley publishes in a variety of print and electronic formats and by print-on-demand. Some material included with standard print versions of this book may not be included in e-books or in print-on-demand. If this book refers to media such as a CD or DVD that is not included in the version you purchased, you may download this material at http://booksupport.wiley.com. For more information about Wiley products, visit www.wiley.com.

Designations used by companies to distinguish their products are often claimed as trademarks. All brand names and product names used in this book and on its cover are trade names, service marks, trademark or registered trademarks of their respective owners. The publisher and the book are not associated with any product or vendor mentioned in this book. None of the companies referenced within the book have endorsed the book.

Limit of Liability/Disclaimer of Warranty: While the publisher and author have used their best efforts in preparing this book, they make no representations or warranties with the respect to the accuracy or completeness of the contents of this book and specifically disclaim any implied warranties of merchantability or fitness for a particular purpose. It is sold on the understanding that the publisher is not engaged in rendering professional services and neither the publisher nor the author shall be liable for damages arising herefrom. If professional advice or other expert assistance is required, the services of a competent professional should be sought.

Library of Congress Cataloging-in-Publication Data
Palmer, Alan H.
  Talk lean : shorter meetings, quicker results, better relations / by Alan H. Palmer ; on the basis of original ideas and a framework conceived and developed by Philippe de Lapoyade ; with contributions from Clement Toulemonde.
     pages cm
  Includes index.
  ISBN 978-0-857-08497-2 (pbk.)
  1. Business communication. 2. Communication. 3. Business meetings. I. Title.
  HF5718.P343 2014
  658.4'56–dc23
                                                                        2013027980

A catalogue record for this book is available from the British Library.

ISBN 978–0–857–08497–2 (paperback) ISBN 978–0–857–08494–1 (ebk)
ISBN 978–0–857–08495–8 (ebk)

Cover design: Parent Design Ltd

Set in 10/13.5 pt Adobe Caslon Pro by Toppan Best-set Premedia Limited, Hong Kong

For my wife and children, Sarah, Katie, Alexander and Lizzie, and for my sister, Diana

CONTENTS

PREFACE

Try the following simple experiment: ask a dozen people in your circle of friends, acquaintances and colleagues, with as much diversity as possible when it comes to nationality, culture, sex, age, profession, social class and management level, to answer this question:

> *"If someone – a colleague, a client, a boss, a subordinate, a supplier, a spouse, a friend, a lover, a stranger – approaches you to ask you for something or to tell you something, how do you want things to be said, how do you like the other person to speak to you?"*

Write their answers down in two columns, one for "Content" and one for "Manner".

I am confident that their answers will be almost exactly the same as those in the chart overleaf:

Content	Manner
clear	polite
direct	calm
straight to the point	respectful
simple	courteous
precise	warm
concise	with humour if possible
concrete	etc
etc	

My confidence is born of hard data. Across 20 years, in the course of teaching people how to deal more effectively with others, trainers at our company, Interactifs, have posed this question to over 60,000 people around the world, of all ages, of both sexes, in diverse functions, at many different hierarchical levels and in all kinds of industries (and we continue to pose it). The answers – the ones you'll find above – are ALWAYS the same. An ability to speak in a way which is consistent with these answers is the essence of "talking lean".

Note that the question is about what people would like, not what actually happens. There is clearly a huge paradox at work here. Although human beings can identify very rapidly how they like to be spoken to and therefore, by extension, how other members of the human race may also like to be spoken to, very few people are consistently able to be direct without becoming brutal or unpleasant; or to be courteous without being submissive or manipulative. They are confronted with what they see as a stark choice between being direct or being polite.

Resolving that dilemma is the subject of this book.

ACKNOWLEDGEMENTS

The approach for "talking lean", described in this book, for dealing more naturally and more effectively with other people, is called the Interactifs Discipline®. It is the fruit of many years of study, observation and reflection carried out by Philippe de Lapoyade, founder of the Interactifs company and my "Master" (please think "Zen" or "Jedi" and not "50 Shades of Grey"!) in every aspect of the Discipline. Without this work, my canvas would be blank; and I am happy to acknowledge my debt to Philippe, both for inspiring me to pick up my (figurative) pen and more broadly for changing the way that I interact with my fellow human beings and for increasing the pleasure which I derive from doing so.

Philippe and his colleagues at Interactifs have been teaching the Interactifs Discipline for almost 25 years to companies of all sizes, at all levels, from the executive board to the showroom sales force, and in many countries and many languages around the world. An up-to-date list of our clients, who include many blue-chip multinationals, is available on our website, **www.interactifs.com**.

The Interactifs Discipline is protected under the laws of intellectual property, but Philippe has given me permission to describe it in these pages. Many of the examples and anecdotes cited were originated by Philippe or by other colleagues at Interactifs; but this text remains my own and any errors, either of commission or omission, are mine and mine alone.

As the originator of the Interactifs Discipline, Philippe could certainly write a more complete and definitive book on the subject than I; and I am optimistic that one day he will. In the meantime, I offer this volume to English-speaking readers, with thanks to Philippe and to all my colleagues at Interactifs, both past and present, for having introduced me to the Interactifs Discipline and for having helped me to achieve some level of competence in practising and teaching it.

In particular, as well as Philippe, I want to thank the following colleagues who have contributed to my apprenticeship: Laurent Allain, Philippe Beraud, Fred Blind, Alain Champagne, Mark Elliott, Alain Garnier, Nathalie Hammou, Sara Lucet, Patrick Maito and Annabella Silverio.

Special thanks are due to Clément Toulemonde, my fellow director in Interactifs UK, for his tireless re-reading, his invaluable advice, feedback and suggestions and for his rigorous editing of the text.

PART ONE

INTRODUCTION

1

What the book is about and who it's for

Consider the following probably all too recurrent situations.

- You don't like the way your new boss is managing you. He's constantly looking over your shoulder, checking not just whether you meet your objectives but also how you do so. He has criticized you in front of your subordinates and has taken decisions which affect you without discussing them. He's succeeded in thoroughly demotivating you but doesn't appear to be aware of that. You need to tackle him about this.

- At a conference, you spot a prospect you've been unsuccessfully chasing for six months. The person he's drinking a coffee with during a break suddenly excuses herself to answer a call, leaving your prospect alone and five feet away from you. Now's your opportunity!

- You're a senior management consultant. At the end of an assignment, your client has asked you to carry out some additional analyses. You agree to do so at no extra cost, but the analyses are more complicated than you envisaged and your team has spent a considerable amount of extra time interrogating the data. You think you're justified in asking for an additional fee but feel uncomfortable doing so after the work has been done rather than before. You hesitate before making the call.

- Someone you manage makes invaluable contributions to the project you're working on together, but he's always late for your team meetings and his lateness is starting to become contagious. You've already explained to him the problems this poses but it hasn't made any difference. Yesterday your boss came to the team meeting. She was singularly unimpressed by the fact that the meeting started 10 minutes late and asked you afterwards to sort things out. You need to do so.

- You've had a fire overnight on your production line and you've just been told by your operations manager that a big order to a major client can't be delivered on time. Now you need to pick up the phone and give the client the bad news.

- You're a front office manager in conversation with a customer. You feel the customer is being gratuitously rude to you but you ignore it in the hope of preserving the sale. But the more you ignore the insults, the worse they get. You need to address the situation.

- It's 2 o'clock in the morning. After a party in your flat, a member of the opposite sex to whom you are strongly attracted (and not just because it's 2am) has stayed on to help you clear up. Instead, you end up having a deep and meaningful conversation over the last bottle of wine. Your thoughts turn to romance – or at least to lust. Then he/she says: "I suppose I ought to be thinking about getting a taxi." You clear your throat to respond.

Situations like these will be familiar to anyone picking up this book. Who hasn't hesitated before leaping in? Who hasn't, on occasion, failed to leap in at all? Who hasn't had cause to regret the things left unsaid; or the things which were said, but ineffectually or maladroitly? Apart from those of us incarcerated in solitary confinement, marooned, Crusoe-like, on a desert island or pursuing careers as the loneliest of goatherds (and I'm guessing that if you're reading these words, none of those descriptions apply to you) then we all spend most of our lives interacting with our fellow human beings, both professionally and personally – negotiating, selling, influencing, requesting, procuring, transacting, seducing, persuading, resolving; and our happiness and success at practically every level is in large part measured by how effectively we do so.

Dealing effectively with someone else doesn't just mean getting what you want from them. Being effective also means getting the result quickly rather than laboriously. And, even more importantly, it means doing so whilst maintaining or enhancing the relationship with the other person so that they'll continue buying from you, going out with you, living with you, working for you, employing you. It also means maintaining or enhancing the relationship even if, for objective reasons, you don't get the result you want – so that perhaps you'll still have a chance in the future.

It's my view that the "secret" of dealing effectively with other people is no secret – and not just because it's been exposed in the preface to this book. We all instinctively feel greater respect for someone who speaks candidly than for someone who beats around the bush. We trust them more and if their honesty and transparency is also accompanied by courtesy and respect, we are more likely to help them if we can. On the basis of "do as you would be done by", we automatically understand that we will have more impact, generate greater trust and confidence and give ourselves a better chance of the other person listening to us in an open and receptive frame of mind if we can speak straightforwardly and honestly – as long as we can manage to do so without also being blunt and abrupt.

Our instincts are clearly telling us what we should be doing. But how to do so? For there's the rub. The vast majority of human beings are faced with what they see as an insoluble dilemma: to be clear, straightforward and direct, but risk being seen as blunt and brutal; or to be polite, respectful and courteous but incapable of getting to the point. In other words, to have no inhibitions and trample heedlessly on the sensitivities of the listener, or to be a slave to inhibition and tread so softly as to leave no trace.

This is of course a false dilemma, because how can you be truly respectful of other people if you're not also being straightforward with them? This book will suggest ways in which you can systematically square the circle – it will propose principles which will allow you to "talk lean", to be both candid and courteous in every situation. If you apply these principles, you will give yourself every chance that other people will be open and receptive to what you have to say and ready to help you if they can.

Many years ago, I witnessed a scene on the London Underground which has remained vividly in my memory. A young man hanging onto straps near mine was clearly attracted to a girl who had jumped in at the same station – and it seemed to me that his interest was shyly returned. This scenario probably recurs a thousand times a day on the Tube in London and in other cities around the world, but in most cases nothing at all comes of it because neither party finds the courage or the words to say what's really in their mind. (I've noticed recently that rather than seizing the moment, these prospective lovers have started saying what's in their mind the next day in the columns of free commuter newspapers [*Rush-Hour Crush* in the London *Metro* is one such column] – by which time the opportunity has probably been missed, or at the least has now been entirely drained of the seductive power of spontaneity.)

But the young man in question clearly did have both the necessary courage and the words to grasp the moment. After a couple of stops, he spoke up (discretely, but I was an attentive eavesdropper) and a conversation ensued which went something like this:

> **Boy:** Excuse me. Uhhh . . . I apologize if I'm being forward. I've been wracking my brains since you got in to find something original to say. But my mind's a total blank, you're probably going to get out at any minute and the moment

will have gone; so I just want to say that I really like the way you look . . . and I'd like to have a coffee with you!

Girl (reddening but smiling): Oh! . . . I don't know what to say . . . that's quite flattering!

Boy: So what do we do now?

Girl: I don't know! What do you suggest?

Boy: How about that coffee?

Girl: When?

Boy: At the next stop?

Girl: OK! Why not?

The reason the young man's words have stuck in my mind over the years was because they impressed me so much. I was awe-struck – and envious.

He had been spontaneously both straightforward and polite, he had found the freedom to put into words exactly what he was thinking and he did so in a way which was comfortable for him and comfortable for the person he was talking to. He spoke respectfully and generated respect; and consequently he presented himself as someone who was honest, genuine and sincere rather than as a smooth pick-up artist. The conversation was efficient because it quickly produced the result the young man was looking for.

His initiative could just as well have ended in failure if the girl had not been single or simply didn't like the look of him. But he would certainly still have gained her respect (as well as mine) and he wouldn't have spent the rest of the week regretting what he hadn't found the courage to say – to the detriment too of his own self-respect.

This analysis came to me years later with the benefit of 20/20 hindsight. At the time I simply reflected ruefully that some people have a natural gift for communicating which the rest of us can only envy from afar; and that those people will probably be the ones who will have the most fun in life by landing the best jobs, the most appealing dates, the fastest promotions, the most valuable contracts and everything else we'd all like to ask for but don't dare to. And after that reflection, I went back to reading my newspaper and to carrying on my life as a distinctly second-division communicator.

Luckily, 15 years later I met a man called Philippe de Lapoyade who showed me that communication skills at this level can be developed by anyone. Like me, Philippe had witnessed situations in which someone had dared to speak up and had done so in a way that had delivered results and enhanced the relationship. Unlike me, he hadn't simply reflected ruefully that some people are born with those skills and some people aren't.

Instead, he set out to identify, via meticulous observation of his own meetings and those of many others, the verbal behaviour patterns which consistently produce concrete results rapidly and whilst enhancing the relationship. The target of his observation was "effective communication" rather than "effective communicators" because he noticed that we're all capable on our day of effective communication. Great communicators don't possess skills which the rest of us wholly lack; they just manage to deploy those skills more consistently.

It is no surprise that "effective communication" turned out to be communication which was simultaneously both candid and courteous. Where Philippe's exercise contributed huge value was in identifying the "how" rather than the "what". As a result of his observations, he defined a set of simple rules to describe effective behaviour patterns in meetings and conversations so that he could apply them himself, consistently and consciously, rather than occasionally and unconsciously; and so that he could teach others to do likewise. What you are reading is based on the results of that canny piece of reverse engineering.

This book is not unique in addressing the subject of dealing effectively with other people – doing so is after all a pretty fundamental part of being a human being and it is not surprising that the subject has inspired a substantial bibliography. I can't claim to have read every book on the topic, though I have read a good few. Some are simple compilations of the blindingly obvious ("It's a good idea to remember the other person's name" is an example I found recently), the better ones contain good common sense but no framework for applying the common sense consistently, the best contain both common sense and a framework for applying it – but in my (admittedly partial and subjective) view no other book on the subject will give you a framework and tools that are so effective and yet so simple. This is the consequence of Philippe's rigour in condensing and organizing the fruits of his observations into a concise set of easily understood principles which can be summarized on a single page – and at the end of the book, they will be.

As the example from the London Underground suggests, this is a book about seduction, but not in the narrow sense of erotic seduction. It is about seduction in a much broader sense. Seductive behaviour, in both a professional and a personal context, is behaviour which is attractive to the other person, which engenders trust and confidence and so puts them in an open and receptive frame of mind, ready to allow themselves to be taken in the direction in which you have told them you want to take them. Seductive behaviour is necessarily based on transparency and sincerity – the absence of those qualities is unattractive because it creates anxiety and puts us on our guard. Paradoxically, there is nothing less seductive than the behaviour of a seducer. The would-be Don Juan, or the salesman oozing faux charm, both have intentions which are plain, but which invariably remain unvoiced, with adverse consequences for the generation of trust and respect.

What the Book Does

The book will suggest how to *introduce* any meeting or conversation – a sales meeting, a request for a raise, a loan, an investment or a date, the assignment of an arduous task, the extraction of a promise or a commitment, the announcement of bad news – and how to prepare that introduction so that right from the outset, the other person will be curious, open and receptive to your request, ready to listen and to help if possible.

It will suggest how to use your arguments *during the meeting* in a way that will ensure they produce something other than counter arguments. It will suggest how to listen with rigour and precision to the other person and to demonstrate irrefutably not only that he or she has been listened to but also that you have done something with what you have heard. It will suggest how to react verbally to what the other person says in the conversation, how to seize opportunities and overcome setbacks, in a way which guarantees complete consistency between what's going on in your head and what's coming out of your mouth. It will suggest how to ensure that all of the energy during the exchange is focused on achieving your goal or protecting your interests whilst also constructing the required amount of trust and esteem. It will suggest ways of dealing effectively with the situations described at the beginning of this chapter – but it will give you the verbal tools to deal effectively with ANY situation.

The ideas advanced in the book will have a significant impact on the productivity of your meetings at the level of both the relationship and the results.

Some of the approach described in the book is relevant only to meetings and conversations which YOU have initiated (what I will refer to as "outgoing" meetings). Unless you're the one who's called a meeting or initiated a conversation, it's not your role to open it. But many of your meetings and conversations are "incoming", initiated by someone else and for which you can't prepare and can only listen and react. The book will suggest how to be more effective in both outgoing and incoming meetings and conversations.

Much of the book's content may suggest that its subject is primarily dealing with other people in *challenging* meetings, where the stakes are high. By definition, this is the area where the book is likely to be most helpful – and probably the reason you picked it up. But although our approach will help you to tackle tricky meetings more successfully, Philippe is keen to emphasize that his focus in developing the approach was not on solving problems but on constructing results and relationships. To borrow an analogy from another colleague whose passion outside work is growing trees, the approach should not be seen as a way of putting out forest fires, but rather as a way of planting saplings.

Once you've understood and assimilated the approach as it relates to handling challenging meetings, I hope therefore that you will appreciate that everything between these covers can also be practised in easy meetings, to make them even simpler, quicker for all involved and more positive in terms of the impact on your relationship with other people. It will help to reduce the pain you suffer in difficult meetings – but much more importantly it will help to increase the pleasure you derive from all meetings.

What the Book Does Not Do

The book can't – and doesn't set out to – provide a cast-iron guarantee that if you apply the approach you will always get what you want from a meeting. More modestly, it will give you the courage to say what you think and to ask for what you want and, if what you want is obtainable, it will give you the best chance of obtaining it quickly. And if what you want isn't objectively attainable under any circumstances, you will find this out more quickly too and avoid wasting time and energy; and avoid the risk of poisoning the relationship through fruitless argument.

The book will not seek to change who you are; it will seek instead to change what you do with who you are.

It will not seek to impose upon you standard words and phrases. You will be able to assimilate everything between these pages in a way which is entirely consistent with your own vocabulary and way of speaking.

The book will not school you in the dark arts of manipulation. Deliberate manipulation (by which I mean trying to take someone somewhere without telling them in advance where you're trying to take them) can undoubtedly be an effective *short-term* strategy for getting what you want (which is why, regrettably, manipulative behaviour – under different names – is often taught to people in management and sales roles).

Unsurprisingly, most of us dislike being on the receiving end of manipulative behaviour. We usually realize pretty quickly, though often too late, what's happened, with negative consequences for the relationship. De facto, manipulation is not an effective *long-term* strategy if you want to maintain or enhance the relationship and continue getting what you want from the other person. Most of us are also uncomfortable being asked deliberately to manipulate someone else; and in our view, companies should think twice about asking their employees to do things they're not comfortable with, particularly if those things are also of dubious strategic value.

A particularly egregious form of manipulation is the surreptitious application of "techniques" or "methods" to the unconscious mind of the other person. There is a strong belief in many quarters that the most effective way to influence someone else is by working on his or her subconscious. There is no doubt that we all process a lot of the information in a meeting or conversation at an unconscious level – what the other person looks like, how they're dressed, how they speak, the way they hold themselves, the space they occupy and much more; and it is consequently quite possible to influence the other person by working on their unconscious mind. But this is a difficult trick to pull off subtly and without detection. You could never openly admit to using techniques which act on the other person's subconscious – and if the other person ever suspects that you are consciously setting out to work on their unconscious mind, it's likely to be disastrous both for the result and the relationship. The advice in this book is exclusively concerned with working on the other person's *conscious* mind.

Admittedly a lot of manipulative behaviour is applied accidentally rather than deliberately, without ill-will or dishonest intention, but simply through the lack of an accessible alternative. This happens when people instinctively disguise their real purpose when they've got something difficult to say, because they think that if they come straight out with it, they will immediately frighten the other person off – so they adopt a more circuitous route.

Far from endorsing manipulative behaviour, the book will demonstrate that, whether applied deliberately or through force of circumstance, it is unnecessary and counter-productive; and that it is possible to influence and persuade far more effectively without recourse to such behaviour.

The approach on which this book is based and which we teach in organizations around the world is resolutely not called "The Interactifs Technique" or the "The Interactifs Methodology". Instead, we call it "The Interactifs Discipline". We believe the distinction is an important one. This approach is not something which you apply to other people in the expectation that IT will be effective; it is something which you apply to yourself in the expectation that YOU will be effective.

2

All different . . .
and all alike

What you will have acquired by the end
of the chapter:

An awareness of the universal hunger of human beings, wherever they
come from, whatever they do, whoever they are, to be spoken to in a
way which is consistent with the principles exposed in the preface to
this book.

The human race is both extraordinarily rich in diversity and extraordinarily homogeneous. There are around seven billion of us and until cloning becomes a reality, we all remain totally unique. No two of us have exactly the same DNA or the same set of fingerprints (or even, a recent discovery claims, the same-shaped ears). But despite our uniqueness we're also all recognizably members of the same species. A medical student cutting up cadavers will find the same bits in the same places whatever the origin of the specimen; and although our DNA is unique, 99 per cent of it is shared across the entire human race. We all need air, warmth, food and water to survive. We will all die. Our homogeneity is not limited to the physical – we also share basic psychological traits. We like to be loved or at least liked or respected; and we hate being deceived and or belittled.

Many approaches for dealing more effectively with other people focus on the differences between people rather than on the similarities. They identify broad psychological categories (there were 23 of them in a book I read recently which took this route) and ask us when dealing with someone from whom we want to obtain something – a prospective customer, a prospective employer, a prospective mate – first of all to identify, at lightning speed, to which of these categories the person belongs and then to modify our behaviour accordingly.

This seems to me both difficult and dangerous. Trained psychoanalysts spend hours with their patients on the couch before making a diagnosis or drawing a conclusion. Cynics may draw a link between this and psychoanalysts' hourly rates, but cynicism aside, a human personality is a deeply complex thing and it's asking a lot for someone with no psychological training – the average businessman or woman, the average mother, father or spouse, you or me in other words – to make an accurate analysis of someone's personality type within a couple of minutes. Even if you WERE able to make an accurate analysis, IT'S NOT YOUR JOB TO DO SO! You're in a business meeting, not a consultation and you have no legitimacy in probing the psychology of your interlocutor. In addition, if you modify your behaviour based on the conclusions of your analysis, whether it's an accurate one or not, you're now doing something which would make the other person very uneasy if they suspected what you were about.

If you're on a date and find that your body language is spontaneously mimicking that of the other person because you fancy their socks off, that's fine (and good luck with that!). But if you deliberately start mimicking their body language because you read in a book that it'll give you a better chance of seducing them, that's cynical and manipulative and I hope they'll see through you. (Of course if you TELL the other person you fancy their socks off and you're deliberately mimicking their body language because you read in a book that it's an effective strategy for seduction, that makes all the difference. You're no longer being manipulative because you're no longer hiding your intentions.)

The differences between human beings are one of the great riches of the human experience so I'm not going to suggest that you ignore them. But when dealing with other people, I firmly believe that it's a lot simpler to focus on the things that the seven billion of us have in common rather than on the things that make each of us different and unique.

Luckily, as you discovered – or had confirmed – in the preface to the book, it turns out that when it comes to dealing with other people one of the most fundamental points of commonality between human beings is a desire to be spoken to in a way which reconciles candour with courtesy.

You may retort that there's huge variety in the ways in which different human beings speak to you and that very few of those are simultaneously both direct and polite. Remember, the question in the preface was "How do you like to be spoken to?" and not "How ARE you spoken to?" or "How do YOU speak to other people?" Those last two questions would inevitably produce very diverse responses, conditioned by the personality, culture and nationality of the person answering the questions. There are huge differences, both personal and cultural, in the way that people actually do speak to each other. But there's surprising homogeneity in the way that people want to be spoken to. The adjectives in the table in the preface represent *universal human wishes*. But the daily experiences of most people lead us to have very low expectations of those wishes being fulfilled.

Human beings are often so concerned with preserving the relation-ship at all costs that if they've got something difficult to say or to ask for, they end up going all round the houses and can't get to the point. And then sometimes when circumlocution, which is often confused with politeness, doesn't get them what they want, they end up getting frustrated, politeness flies out of the window and they become brutal and harsh – and probably still get nowhere.

Some people – the "bluff northerners" of legend, the "shoot-from-the-hip straight-talkers" – are very good at getting directly to the point, but often at a cost of being perceived as brutal or insensitive. The people on the receiving end know exactly what's expected of them; however, depending on the relative hierarchical relationship, they may end up either carrying out an order, but begrudgingly, or putting a request right at the bottom of their "to-do" list because of the way it was made.

Most people oscillate between these two alternatives, depending on the context, on their mood and on who they're talking to. They may be harsh with their subordinates or family but hopelessly submissive and/or manipulative with their clients or bosses. Unhappily, experience suggests that the more people go to one extreme with one audience, the more likely they are to go to the other extreme with another audience.

Whilst culture is surprisingly absent as a factor when it comes to how people like to be spoken to, it clearly plays an important role in how people actually do speak to each other. Cultural stereotypes are oversimplistic – but they are often anchored in some truth.

The British are usually so concerned with not ruffling feathers or hurting the other fellow's feelings that if we've got something difficult to say we end up beating around the bush by using what we believe to be politeness and courtesy ("How are you today, old boy? Good, good. Do you have a minute? There's a little thing that I wanted to float by you. Would that be all right? Blah blah blah . . ."). In France, the British have a centuries' old reputation for untrustworthiness, distilled in the expression "perfide Albion". This is (hopefully) not an indication of any endemic dishonesty but more a consequence of the British reluctance to say what they really feel or want.

(*The Economist* newspaper once provided a helpful guide for Europeans dealing with British representatives at the EU and interpreting their usually indirect phrases. "Oh, incidentally . . ." should not be understood as meaning "What I'm about to say is not very important . . ." but rather as "I'm getting to the primary point of our discussion". "I agree with you up to a point . . ." does not mean "We're almost there" but "I disagree with almost everything you've said". "With the greatest respect" implies no respect at all and should be interpreted as meaning "You're a complete idiot". It is easy to see how a lack of straightforwardness can result in communications mayhem.)

The Germans, Dutch and Scandinavians are generally assumed to be more comfortable with speaking their minds. But whilst this often means that they have fewer inhibitions, it doesn't mean that they are any more direct. A question like "What the hell was going on in the meeting yesterday?" is more brutal than "Would you mind if we had a little chat about yesterday's meeting?", but it's just as indirect with regard to the speaker's wants. Many Asian cultures put far more emphasis on social harmony than on individual needs – to the extent that however much the situation requires it, some Asians are reluctant to pronounce the word "no" in case it results in a loss of face for the other person. They will find it uncomfortable to be told "no" themselves for the same reason.

The approach described in this book is anchored in the premise that if you took the time to ask the person you're dealing with – whatever the context, whatever the relationship, whatever their age, sex, relative hierarchical position, nationality or culture – how they'd like you to speak to them, you could be confident that they would answer: "clear, direct, straight to the point, concrete, precise and concise, as long as you're also polite, courteous, respectful and calm."

This is emphatically not the same as recommending that what you say in a given context will be exactly the same regardless of the identity of the person to whom you're talking, or that one reader of this book should say the same as another who applies the principles in identical circumstances. There will be significant differences in the verbal outcome as a function of your own cultural background, of how well you know the other person, of your relative hierarchical level, of your degree of cultural homogeneity and so on. Whilst all human beings carry the same range of emotions within their heads, what provokes these emotions – and their intensity – will vary significantly from culture to culture and from individual to individual. My ambition for the book is to suggest standards of behaviour in meetings and conversations which will increase your effectiveness – and certainly not to impose standardized behaviour.

Chapter Summary

- When trying to deal effectively with other people (in terms of both the results and the relationship), it's simpler to focus on the similarities between human beings rather than on the differences.

- From a communications perspective, the most important similarity among disparate individuals is the universal wish of human beings to be spoken to in a way which marries directness, concision and clarity with respect, politeness and courtesy.

- It follows that speaking in this way in a meeting or conversation is most likely to put the other people in the frame of mind you need them to be in to have the productive and comfortable conversation you want.

- Despite this universal wish and what it implies in terms of common standards, most human beings do not consistently speak to other human beings in the way in which they would like to be spoken to.

PART TWO

STRAIGHT TO THE POINT IN LESS THAN A MINUTE: OPENING YOUR MEETINGS AND CONVERSATIONS

3

The benefits of straightforward, straightaway

What you will have acquired by the end of the chapter:

An acute consciousness of the differences, in impact and in likely productivity, which can be achieved by opening a meeting in a way which is straightforward, straightaway.

A financial advisor has, on the recommendation of one of his existing clients, John Smith, secured a first meeting with a wealthy prospect. He's shown into the prospect's office and mentally assesses the square footage of the floor, the thickness of the carpet, the size of the desk and the plushness of the chair he's invited to sit in. After some chit-chat about the weather, the difficulties of getting a taxi in the rain, whether he wants tea or coffee, if he takes milk and sugar, he opens his briefcase, takes out some papers and gets down to business:

> **Financial advisor:** Well, first of all thanks very much for agreeing to see me. I'm delighted to be here. I was hoping today that we could at least get to know each other a bit – and I've also brought along some material describing some of our industry-leading products which I'd like to take you through. And then perhaps we could discuss some areas where we might be able to help you.

An advertising agency CEO has to announce to an important retail client that, for unavoidable but legitimate reasons, the long-serving account director in whom the client has complete confidence is going to be moving off the account. The CEO has invited the client to pop into his office for a chat after her regular weekly meeting at the agency. He takes a deep breath and kicks off:

CEO: Thanks very much for popping in. I just wanted to take the opportunity to have a catch-up chat with you to find out how things are going generally and to get a bit of an update on your business. And I also wanted to float a couple of ideas past you about some changes we were thinking of making to ensure we continue to service your business in the best possible way.

A manager has to deal with one of her team members who has many admirable qualities but whose time-keeping leaves much to be desired. It's not the first time the manager has had to bring the subject up and her subordinate has previously agreed to make a bit more of an effort on this front. But yesterday, he was again late for a meeting at which the department head was present, who wasn't impressed. The manager decides that she should "get straight to the point" and says:

Manager: I was really angry about what happened yesterday. Why on earth do you persist in arriving late? You really should understand that this is a problem.

A salesman has found out that one of his colleagues has had a raise at the end of the year, but he hasn't had one himself. He thinks it's unfair and demands to see the sales director. He starts by saying:

Salesman: I brought in more new clients than Jane last year, so can you explain to me why she's had a raise and I haven't?

Meetings like these happen thousands of times a day right across the planet. There will be infinite variety in the ways in which the people instigating the meetings choose to open them, but based on our company's experience of working on similar scenarios with hundreds of people who exercise these functions in real life, the openings I've reproduced above are far from untypical.

Openings like these may sometimes lead to successful meetings, but what we can immediately determine is that none of them is consistent with "talking lean". None respects the universal principle identified in Chapter 2: the desire of person A to be spoken to by person B in a way which is candid, direct, straight to the point, concise and concrete as long as it's also polite, courteous and respectful. And if person B doesn't start a meeting by being all of the above, then they will *probably* reduce their chances of getting the result they want; but they will *definitely* reduce their chances of getting the result quickly and of increasing the esteem in which they are held by person A.

In particular, in none of the openings above has the speaker been explicit about his or her real intentions.

Here's a point which is absolutely critical to the start of your meetings: every minute which passes at the beginning of a meeting before you announce your real intentions will generate either suspicion or caution. If the other person thinks that he or she knows what you want from them but they haven't heard you say it, they will be suspicious of you. If they don't know what you want and you haven't bothered to tell them, they will be cautious and on their guard. Put yourself in the other person's shoes. If you're on the receiving end of a meeting initiated by someone else, you won't be open, receptive and ready to help them if you can, right from the start of the meeting, unless the other person has, also right from the start of the meeting, been completely transparent about their intentions regarding what they want from you.

How CAN you kick off a meeting in a way which gets straight to the point without being perceived as brutal or abrupt, without antagonizing the other person or putting them on the defensive? When the meeting is a delicate one, when you're not sure how the other person may react, or you're worried that he or she may react badly, how can you find the comfort – and therefore the courage – to get your objective out on the table as soon as possible so that the meeting can start producing? How can you ensure that right at the start of the meeting, the other person is fully attentive, comfortable, receptive, curious and ready to listen and help if he or she can?

To examine the risks and rewards of different meeting openings, let's consider each of the examples given at the start of the chapter. Let's begin with the financial advisor who opened his meeting by saying: "Well, first of all thanks very much for agreeing to see me. I'm delighted to be here. I was hoping today that we could at least get to know each other a bit – and I've also brought along some material describing some of our industry-leading products which I'd like to take you through. And then perhaps we could discuss some areas where we might be able to help you".

The advisor is certainly being courteous, but he is not also being candid: he hides behind meaningless diminutives (". . . get to know each other a bit . . ."); he's locked firmly in the virtual world of the imperfect and the conditional tenses ("I was hoping we could . . ."); and above all he is masking his real intentions (he is unlikely to be satisfied with just a discussion). He understandably wants to be seen as polite and respectful by an important potential customer – but in starting the meeting like this, at best he risks being seen as completely unremarkable and forgettable (any sales person on earth is capable of starting a meeting in this way – and most do). At worst, he risks being seen as untrustworthy because he hasn't been open about what he really wants.

The financial advisor is unlikely to have set out to be duplicitous and it's improbable he'd consider himself to be so; but he is at least guilty of lying by omission. His intention is not "to get to know each other" but more probably to make a favourable impression on the prospect. His intention is not "to go through material . . . describing . . . our products" but more probably to hear the other person say there's a product in there which interests him. His intention is not "to discuss some areas where we might be able to help", but more probably to have identified at least one possible area for collaboration. If these are his intentions, he should say so. He will appear both bolder and more trustworthy in the eyes of the prospect and he will have successfully differentiated himself from the vast majority of other financial advisors.

Compare the example I gave at the start of the chapter with the following counter examples, in terms of the likely impact that the speaker will make on the listener and the likely consequences for the productivity of the meeting. (I have given three alternatives because I don't want in any way to suggest that there is a stock script for approaching this kind of meeting.)

> **Financial advisor:** I'm very happy that – on the basis of John Smith's recommendation – you've agreed to see me today. In light of that recommendation, I feel that I can afford to be direct.
>
> What I'm looking for from today's meeting is to leave here with a clear understanding of what I and my colleagues at XYZ Bank need to do to have a chance of getting a mandate to manage your wealth, just as we do for Mr Smith. How do you react to that as an ambition for a first meeting?

Or

> **Financial advisor:** I'm conscious that John Smith's recommendation gives me an opportunity today – but it also gives me a responsibility, towards both him and you. And I fully intend to assume that responsibility.
>
> To prepare the meeting, I've put together a presentation on what I believe to be the principal reasons for Mr Smith's satisfaction.
>
> And I'd like our exchange today to produce one thing: for you to tell me at the end of the meeting that you'll be calling Mr Smith to say this was a worthwhile use of your time because you're thinking seriously about placing some money with us right alongside his! How do you feel about that before we move further?

Or

> **Financial advisor:** Given John Smith's recommendation, I'm approaching this meeting with confidence – but not with complacency.

Before meeting you, I gathered together the few elements I have regarding your profile, based on my past conversations with Mr Smith; and I'll validate and complete those along the way . . .

And by the end of the hour we have in front of us, I'd like us to have listed together the different projects you have in mind and your financial priorities for the next five years so that I can come back to you within a couple of weeks with a made-to-measure proposal. What do you think of that approach for the meeting?

You may feel that the words in these alternative openings are not ones that you'd use yourself – and that's fine. I am concerned here with principles and structure, not with vocabulary. I hope that you will at any rate find that these alternatives are straightforward and direct without being brutal or blunt – and if so, that you will look forward to examining the principles and structure behind the openings in more detail in the next two chapters.

What about the agency CEO in the second example? He started his meeting with: "Thanks very much for popping in. I just wanted to take the opportunity to have a catch-up chat with you to find out how things are going generally and to get a bit of an update on your business. And I also wanted to float a couple of ideas past you about some changes we were thinking of making to ensure we continue to service your business in the best possible way".

In this example, the CEO, just like the financial advisor, is assuredly guilty of beating around the bush and of disguising his true intentions. The duplicity is probably more deliberate: the CEO is understandably worried about the client's reactions and has decided on a "softly-softly" approach. But in making this choice, he risks being seen as hesitant and cowardly – and also as manipulative (none of which is reassuring for a client and none of which will therefore serve the relationship).

This is not a "catch-up chat" at all, or an opportunity to "float ideas" that the agency was "thinking of making"; and the catalyst for the meeting is not "continuing to service the customer's business in the best possible way", but the need to deal with some bad news which is not negotiable. Since the important retail client wouldn't be in her role if she hadn't been round the block a few times, she's almost certainly been expecting some kind of bad news ever since the agency head first invited her to pop into his office the next time she was in the building. If the CEO's start to the meeting is anything like the one in my example, the client's BS detector will be going off the scale. She will have noticed the CEO's extreme discomfort and will be wondering what's in store.

If the CEO has bad news to deliver, the sooner he can get it out the better, as long as he can do so without being blunt or brutal. Moreover, the meeting is not just about announcing bad news, it's also, more importantly, about how the client reacts to that news. She can march out of the meeting saying she feels she's been stabbed in the back, or she can react philosophically and constructively. The CEO clearly has a preference between these two outcomes, so why not acknowledge that? The context is uncomfortable for the CEO, but his discomfort is legitimate, so why not acknowledge that too? Doing so will give him the assurance and the courage to say the things that he needs to say.

Compare again the example I gave at the start of the chapter with the alternatives below:

> **CEO:** Jill, I feel like a climber who's just about to fall and knows he won't die but might just break a leg. I asked for this meeting today because I need to know what we at the agency will have to do to ensure no damage to our relationship with you, despite the fact that, for entirely unavoidable reasons which I'll lay out for you in detail, we're going to be moving Simon off your account.

Or

> **CEO:** Jill, I feel that I'm going to need to count on your understanding today. I've got to tell you that, for reasons

which in all events are unavoidable, we're going to have to move Simon off your account within a couple of months. I've thought long and hard about how best to handle this to minimize disruption – and what I want today is for us to agree on a transition plan which works best for everyone. How do you feel about that?

Or

CEO: Jill, I'm aware that what I'm going to say will come as a shock to you, but I've made a conscious decision to get things straight out on the table. For reasons I'll explain to you in detail in a moment, we have no choice but to transition Simon off your account over the next couple of months. In that context, I want today to introduce you to Jane Brown, the Account Director I'm recommending as a replacement – and once you've met her, I hope that you'll endorse my choice and that you'll promise to give Jane every opportunity to succeed in the role. How do you react to that?

What about the manager dealing with her talented but unpunctual subordinate? In my third example she kicked off with "I was really angry about what happened yesterday. Why on earth do you persist in arriving late? You really should understand that this is a problem".

At first sight, this opening seems more direct than those used by the financial advisor or the agency CEO in the original examples. It appears to get very quickly "to the point" – but only the *subject* of the meeting has been identified quickly; the intended *outcome* of the meeting, the desired finished product, remains undefined. The subordinate will undoubtedly and immediately understand IMPLICITLY that what is required of him is to be on time in the future. But among the thousands of people to whom we posed the fundamental question which is the subject of Chapter 2, not a single one told us that they liked requests to be made "implicitly". "Explicit" will always (by definition) be clearer than "implicit". As long as "explicit" is accompanied by politeness and courtesy, it will always be more efficient and more likely to put the other person in a receptive frame of mind. And whilst the speaker's intention remains implicit, it is all too easy for the other person to pretend he doesn't know what's required of him.

As well as leaving what she really wants unsaid, the manager has focused solely on her past emotions and adopted a condescending tone. She risks being seen as aggressive or patronizing by her subordinate, with little respect for him. By taking the meeting into an unsatisfactory past, she is likely to provoke either meek submission or confrontation, depending on the subordinate's character. Her anger concerning what happened yesterday is certainly real and it may be an important factor in the negotiation – but its place is later on. Her question ("Why on earth do you persist in arriving late?") is at best not a real question (she gives him no chance to answer), at worst something which risks producing the precise opposite of what she wants, i.e. a justification for lateness in the past rather than a promise to be on time in the future. If she's asking herself how she can resolve this situation without a confrontation, she should just say so.

Consider these alternatives.

> **Manager:** John, how can I be sure that I can count on your punctuality in the future without it leading to a confrontation between us?

Or

> **Manager:** I'm worried that we won't be able to resolve this situation without arguing but I hope that won't be the case. I've been thinking about our past conversations and then about what happened in the meeting yesterday. And in consequence, today I need you to look me in the eyes and promise me that from now on you WILL be on time for meetings. What do you think?

Or

Manager: John, I'm determined to resolve this issue once and for all, even if I'm conscious of taking a hard line. I have decided that your punctuality at meetings is no longer negotiable. Now that you know that, what do we do?

Or

Manager: John, I'm probably being a pain in the backside for you but I don't feel I have a choice. I consider that our last meeting on this subject was a failure; and today, my sole objective is to see you leave my office in a good mood despite your having just learnt that from now on your punctuality for meetings is no longer negotiable. What do you think?

Lastly, what about the salesman who didn't get a raise? He started his meeting by saying "I brought in more new clients than Jane last year, so can you explain to me why she's had a raise and I haven't?"

Like the manager above, the salesman gets quickly "to the point" with regard to the *subject* of the meeting – but not with regard to his desired *outcome*. Like the subordinate above, the salesman's boss will instantly know IMPLICITLY what the salesman wants, but (cf. Chapter 2) he would have greater respect for the salesman if he stated it EXPLIC-ITLY. The salesman's attitude, if he establishes himself as a competitor to his colleague, risks being seen as a provocation because it requires his boss to justify himself. The question "Why's she had a raise and not me?" will probably produce an explanation as to why this has happened, which is surely not really the direction in which the salesman wants the meeting to go. If he instead wants a definition of what he needs to do to get a raise soon himself – why not start by asking that?

Consider these alternative openings:

Salesman: Peter, I know that I risk coming over as a pushy little sod – but I need to understand what I have to do to

35

ensure that at the end of the next quarter, I get a raise to match Jane's.

Or

Salesman: Peter, what can I do next quarter to get a raise to match Jane's, without this request being a career-limiting move for me?

Or

Salesman: Peter, you may well decide to sling me out of the room on my ear but I've decided to take that risk. This is about the end-of-year raise. I've looked at all the numbers comparing my performance to Jane's in duplicate, triplicate and quadruplicate – and I want to leave your office having heard that you've decided after all to give me a raise in line with hers.

I am probably guilty of overlabouring this point and I only do so because of the importance I attach to it: none of the alternatives suggested above is intended as a model script to be followed religiously should you ever find yourself in similar situations. Indeed there is no such thing as a "model" opening because even for very similar situations, the choice of words and phrases will depend on the context, the relationship and the personality. It is not my intention to impose on you a methodology where problem A always requires solution X, but to give you the principles which will allow you to make your own choices and to find your own effective solutions.

That's the aim of the next two chapters. They will lay out the principles that allowed me to construct the openings – candid, concise, direct, polite, courteous – which I suggested above. They will suggest structures and tools which will help you to respect those principles yourself and to open meetings in ways which will maximize the meetings' productivity. However, you will always be able to do so in a way which is appropriate for the particular context and the particular relationship you have (or don't yet have) with the person opposite and which is consistent with your own vocabulary and speaking style.

Chapter Summary

- Most meetings and conversations are opened in ways which omit to identify the real intention of the person instigating the meeting, with diverse but unproductive consequences: the speaker variously fails to make an impact, appears to be cowardly, creates suspicion or caution in the mind of the other person, fosters confrontation and antagonism.

- Sometimes the failure to reveal intentions at the beginning of the meeting is the result of oversensitivity, an excess of what is thought to be "respect", but which is actually nothing of the sort. True respect for the other person necessarily involves telling them right at the outset precisely what you hope to obtain from them.

- Sometimes the failure to reveal intentions is the result of insufficient focus and a consequent confusion between means and ends, or between broader business objectives and meeting objectives; or of a desire to dwell on causes and consequences rather than moving straight to solutions.

- Opening a meeting or conversation in a way which is straight to the point, precise and clear with regard to your meeting goal, whilst remaining polite, courteous and respectful, will always give you the best chance of the meeting producing concrete results, rapidly and with a positive impact on your relationship with the other person.

4

Begin at the end

What you will have acquired by the end of the chapter:

A thorough understanding of how to define a meeting objective in a way that will significantly increase both your personal impact and the productivity of your meetings and conversations.

A meeting, any meeting, is essentially a production process. It can be compared to a production line in a factory, since a meeting's reason for being is the manufacture of a finished product, a concrete result. When you're designing an efficient production line, you start with the parameters of the finished product and work backwards. The same holds true of a meeting. You should begin at the end, by defining the parameters of the outcome you want the meeting to produce.

In all the examples of meeting openings which I suggested in the last chapter, the speaker succeeded in each case in communicating to the listener, within 5 to 30 seconds, exactly what he or she wanted to obtain or produce as a result of the meeting.

The examples contained clear, concrete meeting objectives; and they also included additional elements which allowed the speaker to announce his or her objective right at the beginning of the meeting in a way which didn't appear to be brutal or blunt. Starting a meeting or conversation in an effective manner involves two distinct but complementary skills:

1 Defining a concrete goal for your meeting in a way that will maximize the chances of the meeting being productive, in terms of both the results obtained and the impact on the relationships.

2 Finding a way to announce that goal straightaway at the beginning of the meeting in a manner that is comfortable for you and for the other person – i.e. without bluntness – and which consequently will give you the best chance of ensuring that the other person starts the meeting in an open, curious, positive and receptive frame of mind.

This chapter will focus on the first of these skills. The next chapter will focus on the second.

I'm confident that you will be familiar with the notion of setting an objective before having a meeting. If I supposed otherwise, I would probably induce rolling of eyes and dark mutterings about grandmothers and sucking eggs or "management 1.01". But whilst it may be common practice to set objectives for meetings, those objectives are often defined in a way which is insufficiently precise to serve the productivity of the meeting. In addition, the people setting the objectives often omit to announce their chosen objectives right at the start of the meeting, either through a failure to impose upon themselves the necessary discipline or because they feel they lack the necessary licence.

Sometimes the instigator of a meeting may THINK they've announced their objective for the meeting, but too often they confuse means with ends; or they confuse meeting objectives with broader business objectives. In either case, they will have failed to define an objective which is MEASURABLE AND/OR OBSERVABLE AT THE END OF THE MEETING.

Sometimes the instigator hasn't taken the time to think really hard before the meeting about what he or she wants to obtain from the other person in the meeting; or what he or she wants to obtain from the meeting with that person. They are therefore unable to announce a clear objective.

Sometimes the instigator HAS taken the time to think really hard about what he or she wants to obtain, but feels unable to announce this explicitly to the other person. He or she may therefore announce one objective for the meeting but actually pursue a different, unannounced, objective; or fail to announce an objective at all.

I will suggest below very specific ways of defining and formulating concrete, measurable meeting objectives which will contribute significantly to the productivity of the meeting.

Means versus Ends

I used an example at the beginning of the last chapter in which a financial advisor restricted himself at the beginning of his meeting to announcing that he was hoping "we could get to know each other a bit", he had brought along some material which "I'd like to take you through", he wanted "to discuss some areas where we might be able to help you".

Who can honestly say that they've never started a meeting in similar vein? Who can't plead guilty to: "My goal today is to review progress on . . .", "I'm here to discuss XYZ with you", "My objective is to take you through our credentials . . .", or "I'm hoping we can explore some areas of common interest . . ."?

All of the examples above are expressions of the *means* which you intend to deploy *during* the meeting rather than of the *final outcome* you want to obtain *at the end of the meeting*. The acid test of "means" versus "ends" is that all of the examples quoted above can legitimately be followed by the question "With what objective?". For example: "I want us to get to know each other a bit", "With what objective?"; "I'd like to take you through [some material]", "With what objective?"; "Perhaps we can discuss some areas where we might be able to help you?", "With what objective?"; "My goal is to review progress on . . ." "With what objective?".

A further test of means versus ends is to ask yourself: "What does my company actually pay me for?" The answer is unlikely to be "to discuss", "to review", "to present" or "to explore"; and much more probably to be "to have obtained", "to have agreed", "to have found", "to have defined".

Announcing the means you propose to deploy rather than the end you wish to achieve may still sound professional, but it is singularly lacking in impact. Any salesman is capable of starting a meeting by saying "I'm here to present our new product in detail". Any manager is capable of starting a meeting by saying "I want to review progress on the project". The person opposite may, for all the usual reasons, feel unable to say what's actually happening in his or her head listening to openings like these, but it is likely to be: "And with what ultimate goal?" or "So what?". Remember from the last chapter that until you announce your final goal for a meeting, you will either be producing suspicion in the other person's head (if he thinks he knows what you want) or caution (if he has no idea what you want).

"Selling", in the broadest sense of the term (which includes getting anyone to do anything), is first and foremost about creating trust and behaving in an appealing manner. Being explicit about your intentions in a meeting is an essential first step in creating that trust. It's a pity that many people who are paid to sell or to manage so often do exactly the opposite (usually because that's what they've been taught to do).

Business Objectives vs. Meeting Objectives

When I recently asked a real-life financial advisor in a seminar about her objectives for a first meeting with a prospect, she replied "I want the client to give us his portfolio to manage!" I asked her if she expected that to happen at the end of this first meeting. "No!" she replied, "These things take time, you have to build trust first, establish a relationship, and only once that happens is there any chance of getting the business"; which led me to conclude that what I'd heard first ("give us his portfolio to manage") was a longer-term *business objective* rather than a specific objective *for this meeting*.

A *meeting objective* has to be something that is measurable and/or observable *at the end of the meeting*. It can't be something which is only measurable and/or observable next week or next month or next year, because you need to leave a meeting knowing whether or not you've achieved your meeting goal.

There's clearly a close relationship between a meeting objective and a business objective – but they're not the same thing. A meeting is a stepping stone on the way towards achieving a business goal and each meeting should get you as far as is realistically possible towards achievement of your business goal (so that you get there in as few steps – meetings – as possible).

Sometimes a meeting goal and a business goal WILL be the same thing. In some circumstances, you CAN expect to achieve your business goal even at the end of a first meeting. Imagine for example that the financial advisor had been meeting a prospect for the first time not simply as a result of a broad recommendation from another client, but because the other client had said: "You have to go and see my friend Mr Brown. He's urgently looking for help to deal with an unexpected inheritance and he's unhappy with his bank". In that case, the financial advisor might reasonably hope to leave the meeting with a mandate to manage the inheritance.

But without such a promising introduction, it's normally unrealistic, because of the importance of relationships when it comes to managing money, to suppose that a first meeting with a prospect will produce the coveted mandate. But there will hopefully come a time, perhaps one or two meetings down the road, when the financial advisor's business goal and his meeting goal coincide, because he CAN realistically expect that at the end of the meeting the client asks him to manage his portfolio.

Confusing a meeting objective with a business objective BEFORE the two genuinely coincide risks making you look overambitious or even greedy if you announce it ("I'm hoping you'll ask me to manage your portfolio"); but more probably will result in you keeping your objective to yourself and therefore starting the meeting without a clearly defined goal.

I suggested to the real-life financial advisor mentioned above that she ask herself what concrete end result she can realistically hope to achieve at the end of a first meeting with a prospective client, which will allow her to leave the meeting satisfied that she is on track towards achieving her ultimate business goal in as few steps as possible. In defining her meeting goal, she should seek the right balance between "ambitious" and "achievable". How far towards her ultimate business goal can she realistically expect to have gone at the end of this first meeting?

There is no universal answer to that question; there will be individual answers for individual meetings between financial advisors and prospective clients which will depend on the personality of the advisor, his experience and the profile of his firm, on whether the meeting has been organized via a personal recommendation, via a cold call or at the initiative of the prospect, on the strength of the personal recommendation if there was one, on what the advisor has been able to find out about the prospect and so on.

I suggested in the last chapter a number of possible alternative objectives for a financial advisor meeting a prospect for the first time on the basis of a referral:

"What I'm looking for from today's meeting is to leave with a clear understanding of what I and my colleagues at XYZ Bank need to do to have a chance of getting a mandate to manage your wealth, just as we do for Mr Smith".

Or

"I'd like our exchange today to produce one thing: for you to tell me at the end of the meeting that you'll be calling Mr Smith to say this was a worthwhile use of your time because you might just place some money with us right alongside his!"

Or

"By the end of the hour we have in front of us, I'd like us to have listed together the different projects you have in mind and your financial priorities for the next five years so that I can come back to you within a couple of weeks with a made-to-measure proposal".

There are many other possibilities, which, like the examples above, will be ambitious and yet achievable (although in reality only the person calling the meeting can decide what, in the particular context, is the right balance). Whatever objective he or she chooses, it must be, like those above, a meeting goal rather than a business goal. It must be something which will happen (or not) at the end of this meeting, and not next week or next month. It will consequently be clearly measurable and/or observable by all. It must be an end and not a means. It must be the result of a process and not the process itself. Objectives like those suggested above are the equivalent in a meeting of the tangible product which drops onto the pallet at the end of a production line.

"That's Exactly What I Want to Happen!"

The real-life financial advisor I mentioned above told me that the most important challenge for her in a first meeting with a prospect was building a relationship. It can be supposed that the establishment of a relationship is a pre-condition for achievement of the objectives

I proposed above; but if the absolute priority of this particular advisor with a particular client on a particular day is the establishment of at least the beginnings of a relationship, then she should be explicit about this.

How did she know, I asked her, at the end of a first meeting with a prospect, whether or not she'd established the beginnings of a relationship?

She said that if the client agreed to a second meeting it was always a good indicator. But she also checked the client's facial expression and body language at the end of the meeting. Does he look grumpy or does he look cheerful? How firm is his handshake? Does he look me in the eye?

We were comprehensively in the realm of the "unsaid". Unspoken, or "non-verbal", communication clearly plays an important role in the way that human beings interact with each other; but, whatever anyone will tell you to the contrary, interpreting non-verbal communication is an inexact science (more on this in Chapter 11) and the margin for error is significant.

"How would you feel instead", I asked the financial advisor, "if as well as smiling and looking you in the eye, the prospective client actually said to you at the end of the meeting something like: 'You seem to be someone I could imagine working with. Why don't you come back to see me in a couple of weeks with a concrete proposal?'"

"That would be perfect!" she replied. "That's exactly what I want to happen!"

"That's exactly what I want to happen!" is of course merely a more colloquial way of saying "Those are my meeting objectives!" And if this is what the financial advisor would like to happen, then she should say so:

"What I really hope for at the end of our conversation is that you'll tell me that you feel you've met someone you could envisage working with; and that we fix a second meeting in a couple of weeks for me to come back with some concrete proposals".

Asking yourself: "What do I actually want to happen at the end of the meeting?" rather than "What's my objective?" may help you to distinguish more easily between means and ends, between meeting objectives and business objectives.

The Two Types of Meeting Objective

If you think closely about the kinds of things you may want to actually happen at the end of a meeting, you will soon find that there are broadly only two possibilities:

- EITHER you want the other person to DO something or SAY something or THINK something ("what I want from that person in the meeting").

- OR you want yourself and the other person to have PRODUCED something together ("what I want from the meeting with that person").

Let's look at these two options in more detail.

"My Objective Is that YOU . . ."

The first type of outcome above is an *objective of influence*. Through what you say or show or explain or present or expose during the meeting, you will have influenced (and not manipulated) the other person to take a particular position at the end of the meeting; and the other person will demonstrate that he or she has taken this position by SAYING something or by DOING something. (If you want them to THINK something, you will only be sure that they are thinking it if they actually SAY that they're thinking it.)

This objective from Chapter 3 is an *objective of influence*:

> *"I'd like our exchange today to produce one thing: for you to tell me at the end of the meeting that you'll be calling Mr Smith to say this was a worthwhile use of your time because you might just place some money with us right alongside his!"*

"My Objective Is that WE . . ."

The second type of outcome is an *objective of production*. This is what you want the two of you (or three, or four etc.) to have manufactured together by the end of the meeting, whether this is to have agreed something together, to have defined something, to have drafted something and so on.

(Other verbs you may find yourself employing to express this kind of objective include: "I want us to have listed . . .", "I'm hoping that we will have drawn up . . .", "we will have filled in . . .", "we will have fixed . . .", "we will have found a solution to . . .", "we will have written . . .", "we will have organized . . .", "we will have constructed . . .", "we will have arranged . . .", "we will have resolved . . .", "we will have composed . . .".)

This objective from Chapter 3 is an *objective of production*:

> *"By the end of the hour we have in front of us, I'd like us to have listed together the different projects you have in mind and your financial priorities for the next five years so that I can come back to you within a couple of weeks with a made-to-measure proposal".*

I gave an example earlier which combines an *objective of influence* with an *objective of production*:

"I'm hoping that at the end of our conversation you'll tell me that you feel you've met someone you could envisage working with; and that we fix a second meeting in a couple of weeks for me to come back with some concrete proposals".

Those with a grammatical bent will notice that most of the examples above use "My objective is THAT . . ." rather than "My objective is TO . . .".

When you say "my objective is TO . . .", you run the risk of confusing means and ends, of conflating what YOU want to do DURING the meeting with what you want to have obtained from THE OTHER PERSON at the END of the meeting. When you say "my objective is TO . . ." then YOU necessarily become the subject of the verb which follows, whereas in reality you need the other person (or people) to be the subject, or at least the co-subject, of the verb. "My objective is THAT you . . ." or "My objective is THAT we . . ." will ensure the full implication of the other person in your meeting goal.

Note for example the difference in terms of *measurability* between: "My goal is TO persuade you to be on time for the weekly meetings in the future . . ."; and "My goal is THAT YOU make me a firm promise to be on time in future for the weekly meetings . . .". The first is process, the second is result. Note also the likely difference in impact on the other person. People generally prefer doing things to having things done to them. They prefer to be the subject of verbs rather than the object.

(The rule favouring "my objective is THAT . . ." above "my objective is TO . . ." is not immutable. When you're a black belt in the Inter-actifs Discipline, then clearly phrases like "My goal is to hear you say

. . .", "I want to have obtained your agreement . . .", "I want us to have agreed on . . ." are fully consistent with the notion of implicating the other person in your meeting goal. But to start with, replacing "My objective is to . . ." with "My objective is that . . ." will help you to avoid confusing means with ends.)

A Meeting Objective Is Always Negotiable

When you announce an objective at the beginning of your meeting, you're being very clear about what you want to happen at the end of the meeting. Once the other person has accepted the principle of holding a meeting in pursuit of this objective, it's just a matter of negotiating how to get there (and later chapters will suggest how to do this).

But it IS a negotiation and, as with any negotiation, the possibility exists that you won't get what you want. So in choosing your objective, you have to be sure that it's something that you're either able or willing to negotiate, something over which the other person genuinely has a choice.

Let's go back to the agency CEO from the previous chapter who had to announce to his retail client that Simon, the star account director, was coming off the account. The reasons were legitimate but unavoidable. (I took this case from real life: the account director in question, whom the agency valued highly, wanted to broaden his experience beyond retail and had announced that if he couldn't do that within this agency, he would feel reluctantly obliged to do so in another agency. So one way or another, he was coming off the account.)

Imagine if the agency CEO had started his meeting with the client by announcing as his objective: "What I'm looking for from our conversation today is your agreement for us to move Simon off the account".

51

The retail client would be legitimate in responding with something like: "Well, I'm sure you have your reasons for wanting to do that and I don't want to make life difficult for you . . . but I'm afraid Simon is really important to us and I need him to stay put".

Cue nervous laughter and hand-wringing from the agency CEO. He will now have to respond with something which, however politely he frames it, boils down to: "Too bad. Because whether you agree or not, he will be moving!" The CEO has suggested that something is negotiable by announcing it as his objective – and then revealed that after all it's NOT negotiable. He has presented a choice and then snatched it away. That's not going to help the relationship.

Whilst Simon's departure from the account is NOT negotiable, the kinds of elements which ARE negotiable are the time frame, the transition plan, the choice of successor, the way the client chooses to work with the successor (begrudgingly? open-mindedly?), the impact of the move on the long-term client–agency relationship and so on.

The suggestions I made in Chapter 3 for the CEO's opening to the meeting all allowed him to be very clear that Simon's move is NOT negotiable and to take the meeting instead into territory which IS negotiable:

> **CEO:** I asked for this meeting today because I need to know what we at the agency will have do to ensure no damage to our relationship with you, despite the fact that for entirely unavoidable reasons which I'll lay out for you in detail, we're going to be moving Simon off your account.

Or

> **CEO:** I've thought long and hard about how best to handle this to minimize disruption – and what I want today is for us to agree on a transition plan which works best for everyone. How do you feel about that?

Or

CEO: I want today to introduce you to Jane Brown, the Account Director I'm recommending as a replacement – and once you've met her, I hope that you'll endorse my choice and that you'll promise to give Jane every opportunity to succeed in the role. How do you react to that?

One more example of the importance of defining an objective which is negotiable (this situation is from the start of Chapter 1): if you run a manufacturing company and a production line goes up in flames, you're going to have to announce to some of your clients that they won't be getting deliveries on the due date. They have no choice about this. The delay is not negotiable. The production line is toast.

The clients DO have a choice about whether they maintain the order or not; they have a choice about whether they accept a later delivery date whilst uttering a curse upon all your descendants or whether they accept it philosophically, assuring you that "s*#t happens"; they have a choice on whether they decide that no-one from your company will ever darken their door again or whether they wish you good luck with the rebuilding and look forward to working with you again soon.

You're not going to call your clients "to give them the bad news" (that's your job, not your objective); you're not going to call them with the objective "I'm hoping you'll tell me you're OK with a later delivery date" because that's not negotiable. You are instead going to call them with an objective along the lines of: "I want you to reassure me that this bad news won't affect our long-term working relationship" or "I'm hoping we can agree on a work-around solution" or "I want you to tell me this doesn't mean we'll be on your black-list for the rest of time" or "I hope we can agree on a new delivery date which is feasible for us and acceptable for you".

"My Meeting Doesn't Have an Objective! It's Just an Announcement!"

There are certain meetings which at first sight seem primarily to involve the transmission of information from one party to another. But to suggest that such a meeting doesn't have an objective – or to suggest that the objective is simply "to transmit the information" – is to suppose that the person doing the transmitting is completely indifferent to how the person receiving the information reacts to it or what he or she does with it. There's an important distinction between "transmitting" information and the other person "receiving" it and understanding it and knowing what to do with it.

Imagine you've restructured your team and you call a team meeting "to announce the restructuring". First of all you need to have decided whether the new structure is negotiable or not. Is the meeting an opportunity to get feedback on the restructuring before making a final decision, or is the decision already definitive? Let's assume in this case that the decision is definitive and you're not prepared to change anything in your plans – all you need to do is to inform the team! Or is it?

Even though your team members have no choices regarding the new structure itself (you've decided that it's not negotiable), they DO have choices in the way they receive the news and in what they do with it. They can leave the meeting certain that they have a complete understanding of how the new structure will work and of what their precise role in it will be – or they can leave the meeting confused and unsure. They can leave the meeting motivated and enthusiastic about the benefits of the new structure and happy to implement it straightaway – or they can leave the meeting unhappy, convinced that yet again management has demonstrated it has no clue about how things really work and determined to drag their feet when it comes to implementation.

You are unlikely to be indifferent between these different possible outcomes. Your meeting goal is not therefore "to inform the team about the new structure". That's your job! Your meeting goal is more likely to be something like "that each of you tells me that you now have a clear understanding of how the new structure will work and what its impact on you will be; and that you'll do your best to implement it smoothly".

With these objectives, which are fully measurable at the end of the meeting (your team will either have told you these things or they won't), you are likely to have a much more productive meeting than if you decide that your objective is simply "to announce the new structure". If you achieve an objective of "announcing the new structure" (let's face it, you're unlikely to fail!) then so what? Nothing will have happened which will either satisfy you or allow you to identify potential problems and resolve them.

Chapter Summary

- When preparing a meeting, start at the end and work back. The first thing you need to do therefore is to define the finished product that you want the meeting to produce.

- In order to be measurable and/or observable at the end of the meeting, a concrete meeting objective should be framed as either what you want the other person (or people) to do or say or think at the end of the meeting; or as what you want the two (or more) of you to have produced together at the end of the meeting.

- A meeting objective should not be confused with the means which will be deployed to achieve the objective, or with a corresponding longer-term business objective.

- A meeting objective MUST be negotiable, i.e. it must be something that you're either able or willing to negotiate, something over which the other person genuinely has a choice.

- Once you've defined your meeting objective, you should announce it to the other person (or people) right at the beginning. Being clear about your intentions will have a positive impact on the productivity of the meeting, in terms both of the concrete results achieved and of the impact on the relationship.

5

And how are you feeling about announcing this objective?

What you will have acquired by the end of the chapter:

An understanding of a simple three-part structure for opening a meeting which will allow you to announce your meeting objective right at the start, in a way which will be comfortable for you and for the other person – and which will multiply your chances of the other person being curious, receptive and ready to listen.

The examples of meeting openings in Chapter 3 contained clear, concrete objectives consistent with the definitions proposed in detail in Chapter 4. The examples also contained some other concise elements; and it was these which allowed the objectives to be announced comfortably for both parties within much less than a minute of the start of the meeting.

Let's now look at these other elements in detail and discover how you can use them to construct a seamless opening which will give you the best chance of ensuring that the other person will be open, curious and ready to allow you to pursue your objective. Ideally, as a consequence of your opening, the other person will (literally or metaphorically) lean forward and say something which, however phrased, means: "I'm listening! Tell me more". At the worst, they will say something which, however phrased, means: "Thank you for your candour, I can't accede to your request, whatever the strength of the arguments you may have". Better for both of you (and for the relationship between you) to find that out at the start of the meeting rather than at the end and after lengthy and wasteful (for both of you) argument.

This chapter will suggest a simple, three-part structure for opening a meeting which will allow you to announce your objective (defined according to the suggestions in Chapter 4) within 5 to 30 seconds in a way which is comfortable for you, comfortable for the other person and which will arouse his or her curiosity and give you the best chance of him or her listening to you receptively.

There WILL be times when you are able to announce your objective comfortably with no preliminaries. The only practices which I hope you will systematically impose upon yourself at the beginning of a meeting are those specified at the beginning of Chapter 4: (i) to have thought carefully about what you want to obtain from the other person in the meeting or produce with the other person as a result of the meeting, and (ii) to announce it to them right at the start.

Sometimes, depending on the choice of objective, on the context in which the objective is being announced and on your relationship with the other person, you will feel comfortable in getting your objective straight out there with little risk of being perceived as blunt or brutal. It's possible to imagine for example, in the case from Chapter 3 of the salesman talking to his sales director, that it's a small, close-knit, informal team in which the boss doesn't place much emphasis on hierarchy; and that the salesman may therefore feel very comfortable just going in to see his director and saying: "Mate – what do I have to do next quarter to get a raise in line with Jane's?"

But many meetings and conversations are far from being emotionally neutral for the person initiating them. By definition, any meeting which is important for you will be emotionally charged. You will often have to obtain things from others which they may either be uncomfortable agreeing to, or disinclined to do so. You may have to announce things which will not be pleasant for the other person to hear. You will be presented with opportunities which thrill you – but which perhaps scare you as well. On a given topic, a close relationship may sometimes make the subject easier to address – at other times it may have exactly the opposite effect.

If you feel very little emotion in a meeting or conversation, then it may be that you are striving for very little, that your objective is not ambitious enough. If it IS ambitious, then it's potentially going to be difficult for you to announce and difficult for the other person to hear. You will need to find a way of communicating it which is more comfortable for you and for the other person – and it is primarily by identifying your emotions, by being explicit about how you feel about announcing your objective, that you will be able to do so.

Traditionally, business books have tended to ignore emotions because "business is business" and "emotions are for wimps". More recently, "dealing with your emotions" has started making an appearance in the literature, probably under the influence of the popular psychology which is increasingly present in modern management approaches. I've noticed that recommendations on what to do with your emotions take two distinct forms:

1. Trying to give yourself the state of mind you think you ought to have in a particular context by "pumping yourself up" or "psyching yourself" or "thinking positively".
2. "Letting it all hang out" – expressing your emotions as a kind of therapy to make you feel better.

In the first case, replacing genuine emotions with artificial ones is rather a severe exercise to impose on yourself. It's also likely to be a waste of time, because, however "delighted to be here" you say you are, however "positive-minded" you try to look, the other person will probably see through the words and the posture to detect the real feelings underneath. Your unconscious body language will betray your conscious body language. There's more on this in Chapter 11.

In the second case, this recommendation is usually thoroughly disconnected from the production process. Dealing with your emotions in a meeting is *only* relevant to the extent that it serves the relationship and the outcome of the meeting.

Let's look at how the Interactifs Discipline can help you to announce your objective more comfortably, both for yourself and for the other person, by acknowledging how you're feeling about that announcement.

EXAMPLE: The New Boss

For the last three months, you've been working for a new boss, Jack, someone brought in from outside the company whom you'd never met before. There's no question about his intellectual capabilities, his deep-seated industry knowledge or his unparalleled functional experience – but you really don't like the way he manages you. You don't feel he trusts you in the way you believe you have a right to expect. He micro-manages you, not just setting objectives and letting you get on with delivering them but telling you in detail how you should go about your job. He appears to keep important information to himself. He has sometimes been scathing about your work. He has contradicted you in meetings in front of your subordinates. He has succeeded in completely demotivating you.

What started as frustration has now reached a point close to meltdown; and either you need to sort the situation out or you're going to have to move on, something you don't feel would be good for your career right now. So you decide to tackle your boss about his management style. You want him to make significant changes in the way he manages you. How can you even broach the subject without antagonizing him and potentially making the situation even worse?

You've bitten the bullet and fixed a meeting for tomorrow morning with Jack. He's asked you what it's about but you've said the matter is delicate and you'd rather tell him once you're in his office. Now you have to sit down and think about how to tackle the meeting. What's your meeting goal and how can you announce it in a way which will increase the chances of the meeting being open and constructive rather than antagonistic and defensive; which will enhance what Jack thinks of you rather than further degrading it; which will increase the chances of Jack actually changing?

Goal of the Meeting with Jack

The primary element in the structure for opening a meeting is obviously the *meeting objective*. Remember that a meeting is a production process and you should begin at the end and work backwards. Everything else necessarily flows from the objective, so it's the first thing you must decide on. Although it will be the first element to be defined in PREPARING your meeting, it needs to be the last thing you say when actually OPENING your meeting. That's because it's to your objective which you will need the other person to react when you've finished your (very short) opening speech.

So what do you want the meeting with Jack to produce? Only you can legitimately decide what you want to get out of any meeting. You will always be confronted by different choices of objective; but if you want to have a concrete and productive meeting, all of the possible choices you consider should be defined exclusively as EITHER what you want the other person to do or say or think at the end of the meeting OR what you want to have produced together.

For the meeting with Jack, we can therefore rapidly reject alternatives like: "I want to discuss the way you manage me" or "I want you to acknowledge that there's a problem" – these are both MEANS to ends, not ENDS in themselves. We can also reject "I want you to change the way you manage me" or "I want us to work together differently" because these are things which may (or may not) happen in the days, weeks or months to come, but which will certainly not happen by the end of the meeting.

Something like "I want you to promise me that you'll change the way you manage me" IS measurable at the end of the meeting – but what does "change the way you manage me" mean? Jack can promise to change the way he manages you, but you could like the new way even less than the old way. It's insufficiently precise. In particular, you need to be sure that you choose an objective which will necessarily satisfy you if you achieve it.

You have clear ideas about the changes you want – no micro-managing, no criticism in front of subordinates, more trust and so on – therefore you might be tempted to say "I want you to promise me you'll stop micro-managing me, stop criticizing me in front of my subordinates and show me some trust". But there are lots of things which can go wrong with this. You're already giving arguments, going into detail of what's wrong – and Jack can and probably will disagree ("I only criticize you when you deserve it, which is far too often!"). You'll already be in a cycle of argument and counter-argument.

Jack is especially likely to disagree if you make reproaches about the past ("Stop micro-managing me") rather than simple requests about the future ("I need you to give me more discretion in the way I choose to meet objectives"). But this level of detail needs to be saved for the body of the meeting, not the start. You may have six things you want Jack to change and if you try to include them all in your objective he won't listen until the end – and even if he does, he's likely to forget the first four.

Jack is also your boss. Although "I want you to promise me you'll stop criticizing me in front of my subordinates" is a negotiable objective in that Jack clearly has a choice, you're giving him a very limited choice: he can either promise or not promise. And as he's your boss, he may well choose not to. And if he does do that, where will you be? This meeting needs to be a discussion, an exchange, rather than the presentation of an ultimatum – but it can still be a discussion with a clear goal.

I feel that what this meeting primarily needs to produce is an agreement between you and Jack on a different way of working together in the future, one which makes you happier and which Jack can at least live with. Let's write this down as an objective for the meeting:

"My objective in coming to see you today is that by the end of the meeting, we've defined a new way of working

together which I'm happier with and which also works for you".

That's a very concrete objective which is likely to satisfy you thoroughly if you achieve it at the end of the meeting. It's measurable (you will either leave the meeting with an agreement on a new way of working or you won't) so you will be very clear about whether you have succeeded or failed.

However, given the strained relationship I described, I suspect you'd be very uncomfortable striding into Jack's office and saying: "Hi Jack. Look, I've come to see you today because I need us to agree on a new way of working together which I'm happier with and which also works for you".

This is assuredly straight to the point – but it may also come over as somewhat blunt. Jack is more likely to recoil in surprise and say "What the hell's up with you?" than to lean forward and say "Let's talk about it". So what can you add which will enable you to announce your objective in greater comfort but still within between 5 and 30 seconds? The primary element which will allow you to do so is an explicit acknowledgement of how you feel about announcing this objective. But there's another element which you can include in the structure of your opening and which will also help you to construct an opening which is as comfortable as possible for you.

"What Did I Do to Prepare the Meeting?"

Before having this meeting with Jack you've almost certainly thought long and hard about the way you and Jack function together – you've thought about what (if anything) you're happy with and what you're not happy with; you've come up with concrete examples you can share if necessary; you've thought about the effect on your motivation and productivity; and you've developed ideas for how you'd like to work

AND HOW ARE YOU FEELING ABOUT ANNOUNCING THIS OBJECTIVE?

together in the future. You can summarize that in a couple of phrases like: "I've been thinking about how we work together and the fact that in some areas I'm uncomfortable with that. I've thought about how that's affecting me and I've brought along some suggestions which I want to submit to you."

Using this element in your opening will arouse the other person's curiosity. It will demonstrate to the other person that the objective he or she is about to hear is not the result of a whim or a caprice but has been carefully thought out and prepared. The element should be extremely concise. It should contain no arguments or justifications, it should include nothing that the other person can already agree or disagree with – and consequently should invite no interruptions.

Now it's time to think about your emotions.

My State of Mind

How does the prospect of announcing this objective to Jack in this context make you feel? And what leads you to feel that way? What is the emotional *consequence* for you of having chosen this objective?

Your state of mind will be absolutely specific to you and specific to *this* meeting with *this* person. How you feel about announcing this objective to Jack will be different from how I'd feel about announcing it to him or how you'd feel about announcing it to someone other than Jack. It's inevitably artificial for me to invent a state of mind for someone else in front of an imaginary meeting.

But given the scenario I've described, I think it's possible that you may feel apprehensive about announcing the objective to Jack because you're worried about his reaction. At the same time, you may be feeling some relief that, despite the worry, you've finally had the courage to have this meeting. So your state of mind is perhaps something like:

*"Jack, I've had to screw up my courage to have this meeting
with you, but I'm actually relieved that I've finally done so"*.

Note that this is NOT how you feel about the situation in general – it's
specifically how you feel about being in Jack's office today, on the point
of announcing to him the specific objective you've chosen.

As a result of the way in which Jack has been managing you for
the last three months, you're frustrated, demotivated, disgruntled and
just plain hacked off. And as a result of that, you have decided to have
a meeting with Jack with the goal of agreeing on a new way of
working together. How you feel about being managed by Jack is the
emotional CATALYST for your meeting. Your state of mind at the
beginning of the meeting is the emotional CONSEQUENCE of
having decided to see him today with this particular objective. Don't
confuse the two.

Also don't confuse how you genuinely feel about announcing your
objective with the bland and insincere social lubricants that are often
used at the start of meetings: "I'm delighted to be here . . .", "I'm
really excited to be having this meeting . . .". These are only acceptable
if you really are delighted or excited . . . and even then, there's a risk
in using these terms that a genuine expression of how you're feeling
will still be heard as a bland social lubricant. So try to find a more
original phrase than "I'm delighted . . ." or "I'm excited . . ." to express
delight or excitement. ("Coming here today, I remember how I felt
when I first learnt to ride a bicycle . . ."; or whatever expression will
appropriately convey YOUR level of excitement.)

We now have three concise elements which together will form an
introduction to your meeting and which will allow you to announce
your goal to Jack in a way that is clear, direct and straight to the point,
at the same time as being polite, courteous and respectful. To build
this opening, I started by defining the objective for the meeting; I
then asked myself what I would be doing to prepare the meeting; and

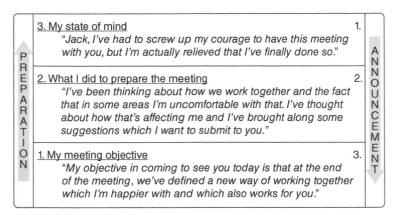

Figure 5.1

I then asked myself how it made me feel to announce this objective, to this person, having done this preparation.

When I open the meeting, I will turn this order on its head and start with my state of my mind.

Schematically, the order of preparation and the order of announcement looks like Figure 5.1.

Taking this from the top down, and reserving the right to make minor adjustments to put this very short speech into spoken language which you're comfortable with, the opening to your meeting will then sound something like:

"Jack, I've had to screw up my courage to have this meeting with you, but I'm actually relieved that I've finally done so. I've been thinking about how we work together and the fact that in some areas I'm uncomfortable with that. I've thought about how that's affecting me and I've brought along some suggestions which I want to submit to you . . . and I really hope today that we can agree on a new way of working together which I'm happier with but which also works for you. How do you feel about that?"

By way of example only, and under no circumstances as a "script" recommendation, here are some other possibilities for how you may be feeling – what your "state of mind" may be – about announcing this objective:

- "This is far from being the most comfortable conversation I've ever had – but I'm hoping that I'll feel it was worth it".

- "The potential importance of this conversation for my career makes me very cautious in approaching it".

- "Our reads on the past few months may be poles apart, so I'm very uncertain about your reaction to what I want to say".

- "Jack, having this meeting feels like going to the dentist: I'm expecting some pain but I'm relieved that I finally made the decision to come".

- "I've chosen to risk being seen as out of order rather than to let things eat me up from inside".

You're free to use this structure in a way which is completely consistent with your way of speaking. The text below is deliberately a caricature, but shows how the structure can accommodate a totally different speaking style:

"Listen boss, I've been sweating like a hooker in a sermon before having this meeting but I'm relieved I finally found the cojones to do so. I've been running through in my mind how we function together . . . and the fact that there's stuff I'm not 100% cool about. I've brought along some ideas I want to run up the flagpole . . . and today I want us to hammer out how we can get off to a fresh start that hits my sweet spot and yours. What do you say boss?"

By my watch, my original opening and the caricature above both take no more than 20 seconds to deliver. These opening seconds are likely to have a significant impact on whether you achieve your objective, on how quickly you do so and on whether in doing so you increase the esteem in which you're held by the person opposite. It's worth investing time to compose something which is clear and succinct and in natural, spoken language which is entirely consistent with your way of speaking – and then to rehearse so that you are completely fluent at the start of your meeting. In my view, every minute spent preparing and rehearsing your opening will save you 5–10 minutes in the meeting. That's an attractive return on investment.

The more you master this very short speech before the meeting, the less likely it is that you will find yourself extemporizing, inserting arguments or positions, which have no legitimate place in front of your objective and which will delay its announcement; or inserting meaningless "filler" words ("basically", "like", "a bit") which will reduce your impact. The only proviso to this is that you should retain the freedom to announce the *actual* state of mind you find yourself in at the start of the meeting, if it turns out to be different from the state of mind you were expecting to be in when you composed your opening.

Crucially, in the example above and in the other examples from Chapter 3, the announcement of your objective is followed immediately by an invitation to the other person ("What do you think?", "How do you feel about that?") to react to your objective. With this, you're not looking instantly to attain your goal at the beginning of the meeting; you are simply looking to obtain the other person's authorization to pursue your chosen objective. If you get permission to pursue your goal (and anything other than "NO!" represents permission) then in my view, within 20 seconds of the start of the meeting, you have already done much of the heavy lifting. You've agreed on a destination; the rest of the meeting is now merely about agreeing on how to get there.

If you refer back to the examples from Chapter 3, you will see that they all (with exceptions which I'll highlight below) respect the structure I've unpacked here. Some of them don't include "what I did to prepare the meeting", but it's not mandatory to use this. The only mandatory element is your intended outcome, your meeting objective.

The examples from Chapter 3 which don't follow this structure are:

"John, how can I be sure that I can count on your punctuality in the future without it leading to a confrontation between us?"

"John, I'm determined to resolve this issue once and for all even if I'm conscious of taking a hard line. I have decided that your punctuality at meetings is no longer negotiable. Now that you know that, what do we do?"

"Peter, what can I do next quarter to get a raise to match Jane's without this request being a career-limiting move for me?"

These are examples of alternative choices for opening your meeting using tools which we will encounter in more detail in Chapters 8, 9 and 10.

Chapter Summary

- Observations of effective verbal behaviour patterns in meetings have allowed us to identify a simple three-part structure which you can use to help you announce an ambitious meeting objective comfortably and right at the outset, in a way which will maximize your chances of the other person starting the meeting in an open, curious, receptive frame of mind, ready to allow you to pursue your objective.

- The three elements – in order of the PREPARATION of your meeting opening – are: (i) My meeting objective; (ii) What I did to prepare the meeting and (iii) My state of mind.

- The order is reversed for the ANNOUNCEMENT of your meeting opening: (i) My state of mind; (ii) What I did to prepare the meeting and (iii) My meeting objective.

- The only mandatory element in the structure is your meeting objective. The other elements are optional and can be used, for example, if they will help you to gain in comfort when announcing an ambitious objective.

- In order to confirm that the other person is indeed ready to allow you to pursue your meeting objective, you should always invite the other person to react to your objective as soon as you have announced it.

PART THREE

TALKING LEAN DURING THE MEETING: THE KEYS TO PRODUCTIVITY

6

Why meetings run rough: the grit in the engine

What you will have acquired by the end of the chapter:

Familiarity with three elements which pollute ALL meetings and get in the way of productivity, understanding and complicity – and some first ideas on how to counter them.

So, using the ideas in Chapters 4 and 5, you've just started your meeting in a way which is clear, direct and straight to the point as well as being polite, courteous and respectful. In consequence, the other person is now more likely to be in a curious, open and receptive frame of mind, ready to listen and to help if he or she can. (Or possibly, despite your best efforts, he or she ISN'T in an open and receptive frame of mind; we must also consider that eventuality and know how to deal with it.) Or perhaps it's not your meeting and instead, someone has phoned you, come to see you, or summoned you to see them. You've listened to their introductory words and now they're waiting for you to respond.

Let's now turn our attention to the body of the meeting, whether it's "outgoing" or "incoming". How do you progress in *your* meeting once you've announced your objective, asked the other person's opinion of that objective and he or she then responds? How can you stay focused on the objective, listen effectively, seize opportunities, deal with setbacks and keep the meeting moving as rapidly and unerringly as possible towards the achievement of the desired outcome? How should you react at the beginning of a meeting which *someone else* has initiated and opened? How can you listen and respond to them in a way which best serves your own interests and which is efficient in terms of the time and energy invested and in terms of the impact on the relationship?

The unhappy truth is that most meetings and conversations are far less constructive and effective than they should be. When two or more people are gathered together in a meeting, there are multiple obstacles to the rapid production of concrete results and contented relationships. Grit from various sources undermines the productivity of the meeting.

The next time you're in a meeting in which you're not a central player, I invite you, instead of surreptitiously checking your emails, to spend some time in the role of detached observer. You will notice how frequently there is a gap between what people are saying and what their expressions suggest they may be thinking, how much the implicit is favoured over the explicit, how hints are dropped, signals given, inferences made, subjects approached obliquely, laterally, elliptically. Depending on the culture and the personalities of those present, it's possible that sooner or later someone will get frustrated that spades are not being called spades and will try to move things along by launching the verbal equivalent of a Scud missile. This will either send everyone else scurrying for shelter, which, in meeting terms, means they will clam up. Or it will set off an escalating arms race where each missile launched is countered by one of approximately double the kilo-tonnage.

When someone says to you during an exchange: "That's going to be a little bit difficult for us to agree to" or "I'll bear your idea in mind" or "I'm slightly disappointed by your figures" or "We'll get back to you", what exactly do they mean? You may have a hypothesis (and the hypothesis will depend very much on the person saying the words and on how they say them) but you're probably as unlikely to be transparent about what that hypothesis is as your interlocutor is to be about his real thoughts.

Cartoonists have long found comic capital in highlighting the discrepancies between speech and thought. In meetings, what people are saying and what they are thinking are too often almost polar opposites.

77

We've all been in meetings which have ended with an exchange like this:

Prospect: "Well thanks very much for coming in to see us". *("Your product sucks and you've just wasted an hour of our lives".)*

Supplier: "It was a pleasure. Thanks for sparing us the time". *("You weren't listening to us and anyway, I know we did a lousy job explaining the benefits of the product".)*

Prospect: "We'll be in touch if we need you. I have your card". *("When hell freezes over. In the meantime, your card's going straight into the bin".)*

Supplier: "We look forward to that". *("We blew this opportunity big time and we're never going to hear from you again".)*

With all this double-speak going on, with few people ready or able to articulate what they are really thinking, it's not surprising that many meetings are inefficient and unproductive. This theme will sound familiar. It's yet again the widespread inability of people to "talk lean", to be both candid AND courteous, which creates two of the most important pollutants in meetings: all the things which are left UNSAID in the meeting but which would serve its productivity if they were said; and all the things that ARE SAID in the meeting but which get in the way of its productivity.

There's a third pollutant at work too. Not only are the participants in most meetings not saying what they're really thinking, they're not LISTENING properly to each other either. They may be pretending to listen, they may even think that they really are listening; but they're almost certainly not listening accurately. They're not even listening properly to themselves. This and the next three chapters will look in more detail at these three obstacles to the productivity of the exchanges in meetings and suggest ways of overcoming them.

UNSAID/SAID

There is obviously a close and complementary relationship between the UNSAID and the SAID. Too much is said which hinders the productivity of the meeting, too little is said which stops the meeting advancing. Through fear of saying things which might displease the other person, we leave unsaid the things which might enhance the relationship. We avoid the explicit for fear of being brutal, but it's the implicit which is the true brute.

The UNSAID in meetings has, self-evidently, two sources: everything which *you're* feeling or thinking or wanting or needing but which you haven't found the courage or the words to say explicitly – and everything which the *other people* are feeling, thinking, wanting or needing which *they* haven't found the freedom or the words to say explicitly and which you haven't encouraged or enabled them to do.

When you feel, think, want or need something in a meeting but can't say so explicitly (or don't know how to), then one of two things will happen. Either you will say something else which isn't explicit, or you will try to pass on your message in an unspoken fashion, through a gesture, your facial expression or body language. For example, if someone has made a proposal, which for various reasons you think is completely impractical, rather than saying "I think this is completely impractical – and I'm prepared to explain why", you may instead end up saying "I'm a little bit uncomfortable with that idea" or "Don't you think that might be somewhat tricky to implement in the current climate?" or perhaps even "Have you been taking your medication?". Alternatively, you may end up saying nothing, but whistling softly and slowly shaking your head; or folding your arms, frowning like thunder and sitting back in your chair.

When, as in the examples above, you try to pass on messages implicitly (either verbally or through different forms of non-verbal communication), your message may or may not get through. If the message DOES get through, then, depending on how you expressed yourself, you risk being seen at best as cowardly or lacking in self-assurance, at worst as duplicitous or unpleasant. If your message does NOT get through, then your views won't be taken into account and you may as well not be in the meeting. You will be seen as ineffectual.

Until something has been said explicitly – and crucially, until receipt of what's been said has been acknowledged – there can be no certainty about what has been, or has not been, communicated. When things are left unsaid, there will inevitably be ambiguity, missed opportunities and the potential for serious misunderstanding.

Human behaviour is contagious, so the more open and explicit you are in a meeting, the more chance you give yourself of the other people being open and explicit too. *But this should not be left to chance.* If you want to have an efficient meeting which produces not only concrete results but also trust and confidence, then you should not just be setting an example by saying exactly what's going on in your head, you should also be actively encouraging and enabling the other person to do likewise. I will suggest ways of doing both of these things in Chapters 8, 9 and 10.

Much of what is SAID in meetings and conversations is said incompletely, imprecisely or plain untruthfully. This is obviously the other side of the UNSAID coin: saying something incompletely, imprecisely or untruthfully means NOT saying whatever it is that would have rendered your statement complete, precise or truthful. "I'm not interested" becomes "We'll think about it", "I want you to sign the contract" becomes "Can we talk about the contract?", "I disagree with you" becomes "I share your view, but . . .", "I won't be getting back to you . . ." becomes "I'll get back to you".

Where the SAID becomes an active obstacle to the progress of the meeting is when people express themselves negligently or artlessly. This can be the result of adopting a position which is fundamentally illegitimate, or of resorting to constructions – such as irony, rhetorical questions or truisms – which implicitly question the intelligence of the other person.

It is only legitimate in a meeting or conversation to talk from your own viewpoint; it is not legitimate to make absolute judgements, judgements on the other person or judgements on what the other person is thinking or intending. In other words, you should try to speak from "I" and not from "you" or "it". All too often a thought in your head like "I disagree with you" or "I have a completely different point of view" comes out of your mouth as "You're wrong!"; "I don't have the budget for that" becomes "That's far too expensive!"; "I'm finding it difficult to work with you" becomes "You're a jerk!"; "I can't accept that" becomes "That's unacceptable!". By always speaking from "I", you will be more consistent with your own thoughts and do more to help the smooth progress of the meeting whilst being just as firm in your position.

Figures of speech such as irony and rhetorical questions enrich the language and can be highly effective communication devices, but their place is in monologue, when you're addressing an audience, and not in dialogue when you're speaking to someone in a meeting (unless the relationship is already extremely close). The definitions my dictionary gives for these terms ("irony: the use of words to express something different from and often opposite to their literal meaning"; "rhetorical question: asking a question to make a point implicitly without the expectation of an answer") make it clear that they both *involve saying one thing but meaning something else*. If you use them in a meeting, the listener is very likely to hear that his intelligence is being questioned. Truisms have the same impact. Consider the following examples:

Client: *I'm not really sure we have the budget for this.*
Supplier: *Don't you see how much money this is going to SAVE you?*

Subordinate: *I'm sorry I was late again.*
Manager: *Are you familiar with the concept of a watch?*

Car buyer: *There doesn't seem to be much room in the back.*
Car salesman: *That's because it's a coupé sir.*

Furniture buyer: *That's too expensive for me.*
Furniture salesman: *Compared to what?*

In all of the responses above, the words "Duh!" or "You moron!" are implicit at the end of the phrase. Even though you have left those words unsaid, they will not be unheard. You have replaced what you're actually thinking with a phrase which is dismissive and insulting for the other person.

Another consequence of imprecise language in a meeting, of leaving unsaid what you really mean and saying something quite different instead, is that energy can be diverted away from identifying the solution to just discussing the problem. The past (which can't be changed) is favoured over the future (which can). If you're thinking "I want you to switch to Blue Cola. What do I need to do for that to happen?" but instead you say "Why do you prefer Red Cola?" don't be surprised if you spend the next five minutes hearing why your competitor's product is so great, and if, as a result, the other person's position is less open than it might have been before.

I will suggest in Chapter 8 a number of simple principles for getting the unsaid said and for ensuring that what IS said is complete, precise, truthful, effective and respectful. But you will only be able to respond effectively if you have listened effectively, so I first need to deal with the subject of listening – and that is the topic of the next chapter.

WHY MEETINGS RUN ROUGH: THE GRIT IN THE ENGINE

Chapter Summary

- Three phenomena recur with alarming frequency in meetings which significantly affect the levels of understanding and productivity: the things which are thought or felt by the participants but which remain UNSAID; the things which ARE SAID by the participants, but negligently or artlessly; and ineffective LISTENING.

7

Don't just listen
with your ears!

What you will have acquired by the end
of the chapter:

An appreciation of the barriers to listening effectively and of the potential costs of ineffective listening in terms of comprehension and productivity; and an understanding of how best to overcome those barriers.

One of the reasons why listening is so difficult to do well is because it seems so deceptively easy. You just open your ears and listen, right? In fact, we all have reflexes and instincts which get in the way of effective listening, but in order to control and counter these, we first need to be aware of them.

Much of the advice and training given to people about listening (typical examples include "Look at the speaker directly", "Avoid being distracted", "Smile and use other facial expressions", "Adopt an open and inviting posture", "Encourage the speaker to continue by saying things like 'yes', and 'uh huh'") could more accurately be described as advice on how to make the other person *believe* you're listening to them, rather than on how to actually listen to them. And advice on what you need to do to be able to "put aside other thoughts" is noticeably thin on the ground.

Suggestions like those above are often grouped under the title of "active listening", which, in addition to all the leaning forward and looking the other person in the eye, also involves "repeating back to the other person what you've heard through paraphrasing". This can certainly be an effective way of demonstrating that you've listened, but if your paraphrasing is inaccurate, it's an equally effective way of demonstrating that you *haven't* listened.

And even when "active listening" DOES demonstrate conclusively that the speaker's words have been heard, the effect can be far from positive. I experienced this recently when I called an IT helpline. I explained my problem to the technician at the other end of the line as follows:

> *"I'm really frustrated because my computer's connected to the router but I still can't access the internet. There's an exclamation mark on the connectivity bars at the bottom right-hand corner of the screen".*

The technician had probably been trained in "active listening" because his initial response down the phone was:

> *"So, if I understand correctly, you're saying that you're connected to the router but still can't access the internet and you're seeing an exclamation mark on the connectivity bars?"*

I had to bite my tongue not to reply "Congratulations! You understand English!". The technician had demonstrated to me beyond all possible doubt that he had listened to what I said. But I was still frustrated. What was missing, crucially, from this demonstration of "active listening" was some sign that he had not only heard what I said, *but had also actually done something with it.*

Imagine instead that the technician had said something like:

> *"Hearing how frustrated you are, I tell myself I'd better help you get rid of that pesky exclamation mark on the connectivity bars pretty rapidly!"*

Or

> *"Hearing your description of what's happening with the connectivity bars, I'm confident that I know what the problem is and that I can solve this pretty fast".*

I would still have had the proof that I had been listened to. But I would also have been reassured that I was not just talking to an articulate parrot or to some sophisticated voice-recording software. I would have known instead that I was talking to someone with a brain, capable not only of listening to information and repeating it back, but also of processing that information. I will describe the principles behind such responses in Chapter 8.

To see how easy it is NOT to listen effectively, let's look at another simple example. Imagine that you recently had a meeting with a client, Jim, to pitch some new product or service. You detailed the numerous bells and whistles which make your product or service so compellingly attractive and left the presentation/documentation/ samples for the client to go through in detail. A week or so later, he invites you back for another meeting and starts by saying:

> *"I've been looking at your documentation. It's very interesting, but at first glance I think this is a little bit over-engineered for our needs. And officially all our budgets are frozen until the end of the year"*.

I have an obvious technical difficulty in using this example in a book because you didn't actually listen to the above speech; you just read it on the page. It's much easier to read effectively than it is to listen effectively. And because you read the speech, you also have it available in front of you to refer back to.

But if you HAD been listening rather than reading, then I am 99.9 per cent confident that what you would have heard and responded to would have been that the product or service is *"over-engineered"* and that *"all our budgets are frozen"*. I say this with no claim to specific knowledge about how you, dear reader, process information, but simply on the basis of what happens in seminars when I or my colleagues ask participants to listen to a short speech like the one above and then to respond to it as if they were in the meeting – and 99.9

per cent of them say something like: "Why do you think it's over-engineered?" or "Why are your budgets frozen?".

The next chapter will cover effective and productive ways of responding in situations like this. But for the moment my theme is listening. And in my view someone who responds to the above speech by saying "Why do you think it's over-engineered?" or "Why are your budgets frozen?" has not listened effectively to the other person – and just as importantly, they haven't listened effectively to themselves either.

There's lots of stuff happening in the client's short speech, some of it potentially positive, some of it potentially negative, much of it rather ambiguous. Ambiguity is a constant in much of what you'll hear from other people in meetings and conversations because of the, by now familiar, difficulty which humans have in "talking lean", in being both candid and courteous – but the ambiguity is often missed. What people on the receiving end of a short speech like the one above are most likely to cling to and process are the negative aspects – because these are what trigger the strongest emotions. The biggest barriers to making this important sale seem to be the over-engineering and the frozen budgets. These are consequently the elements in Jim's speech which will push your emotional buttons most forcefully.

Human beings are likely to retain from a conversation primarily – and often solely – the things which have the most emotional impact on them, the things which cause a shot of adrenalin to start coursing through their veins and which crowd out other information. A related mechanism determines that we can all remember exactly what we were doing on September 11, 2001, but most of us probably don't have a clue what we did on September 11, 2000 or September 11, 1999 because, frankly, not much happened. Those of us old enough can remember what we were doing when we heard that John F. Kennedy had been shot, or John Lennon – but we can't even remember accurately everything we did last week.

Emotion is the first thing which gets in the way of rigorous listening. The second is analysis. In your client's speech, you've heard things which appear to militate against you making the sale, so you start to analyse what you've heard and to think about how you're going to respond and counter-argue. When you hear "over-engineered", you probably start to tell yourself that you disagree, that you're confident you can demonstrate that's not the case, but that in order to do so you need to understand the client's reasons, so that you can then counter them one by one.

When the client's finished speaking, you therefore tell yourself that, as a priority, you're going to need to find out why he thinks your product/service is over-engineered. Whilst you're doing this analysis, your attention will not be properly focused on the rest of the speech. You will probably only hear "our budgets are frozen" – more doom and gloom which you will also start analysing and wondering how to counter.

If you refer back to what Jim actually said, things aren't quite as black or white as they first appear. He hasn't said the product/service is over-engineered, he's said "at first glance, I *think* this is *a little bit* over-engineered for our needs". He hasn't said the budgets are frozen; he's said "*officially* all our budgets are frozen *until the end of the year*". He's also said that he finds the documentation "very interesting". And although he appears to be saying a number of things which sound negative to you, he's nevertheless invited you back for a meeting rather than sending you an email or just ignoring your calls.

The leitmotif running through this book is that people find it very hard to be direct without being brutal so they often take a roundabout approach and try to soften the impact of their words. It's entirely possible that this is what's happening here and that what your client means is that the product/service is way over-engineered (and consequently over-priced) and that he has in any case no possibility of finding the necessary funds – he just hasn't found the words to say that to you without risking hurting your feelings, so he's added a few meaningless phrases to soften the blow.

It's also possible that something entirely different is going on. Perhaps your product/service is exactly what the client's been looking for, but he doesn't want to appear to be too keen because he thinks that if he claims that it's over-engineered there's a chance of negotiating the price down. He also knows that there are always ways of getting round budget freezes, but he will need some creative help from you in order to do that.

And of course between these two extremes of black and white, there are an infinite number of shades of grey. At the moment, you just don't know. The client is anchored in the realm of the unsaid – and so, if your response is "Why do you think it's over-engineered?", are you.

Listening effectively, and by doing so equipping yourself with the raw material which will allow you to respond effectively, involves two distinct steps: (i) listening accurately to the other person's words and then (ii) listening accurately to yourself, to the impact which those words have had on you. Let's look at each step in turn.

Listening to the Other Person

Before you can respond to statements like "I think this is a little bit over-engineered for our needs" in a way which will give you the best chance of achieving your desired outcome you first need to have properly heard the statement in its entirety.

How can you listen more effectively and hear what the other person actually says, rather than retaining only the things which make a strong emotional impact on you? How can you avoid instantly applying your analytical faculties to a phrase you've just heard, with the consequent risk of completely missing the next phrase?

The answer is to TAKE NOTES. This may appear to lack the characteristics of a "miracle solution", particularly if, as I suspect, you already take notes in a meeting. But bear with me because I will suggest changes to the way you take notes which will radically improve your listening.

In a meeting (as opposed to, say, a student lecture theatre or a school classroom) taking useful notes consists of writing down what the other person *actually says* rather than *your synthesis* of what was said. At school or in college, you learned to apply filters when you took notes, to carry out instant mental editing which allowed you to "focus on the essential", to "stick to the facts", to "cut out the padding". You have probably retained this learning and now apply the same approach to note-taking in meetings. In order to listen accurately in a meeting, you need to remove those filters. If in a meeting you try to take down "what's really important" or "just the key ideas", then inevitably you will write down only what appears to be really *important for you* and just the ideas which are *key for you* – and you will probably miss much that is *important for the other person*.

If you'd been taking notes in a traditional way in the meeting example above, there's a strong chance that you would find yourself jotting down "over-engineered" and "budgets are frozen", because these seem to be the key points, the things which appear to be most critical TO YOU in terms of making (or probably not making) your sale. It's highly probable that you would completely miss "it's *interesting*", "*at first glance*", "*a little bit* over-engineered", "*officially*", "*until the end of the year*" because you've dismissed this as so much blah-blah.

It's entirely possible that what the client means by "At first glance" is "This is hard for me to say because I don't want to disappoint you"; it's also possible that "At first glance" means "We haven't actually had time to read the documentation very thoroughly yet". In either case, the fact that the client has chosen to say: "At first glance" makes it important. The order in which people speak and the words they use aren't the result of pure coincidence. The order of a person's speech reveals the way in which the thoughts came to him or her, at that moment and in that context.

Rather than applying filters and writing down what seems to be important *for you*, try instead to write down what the other person actually says, in his or her order and in his or her words. At a minimum, try to write down *the other person's first words*.

This will generate a significant change in the way in which you stock information. If you don't take notes, or if you take notes traditionally and only write down "the key ideas", you will stock information in its order of apparent importance *for you*. If you write down what the other person actually says, you will stock the information in *his or her order*. The fact that the client started his response by saying "It's interesting" doesn't mean that's the most important thing he's going to say; but the fact that he said it, and when he said it, are surely significant. If you've written down the other person's words, you will have a huge amount of raw material to help when you respond.

I warned earlier that it is difficult to conduct an exercise on listening in a book. You can't actually listen to a speech in a book, you can only read it and you will have it available on the page in front of you to refer back to, which makes it much easier to retain. If you write down the other person's words in a meeting, you will enjoy exactly the same benefit. So don't just use your ears for listening – *use your hands too*.

A frequent objection to the simple recommendation of taking notes in a meeting is that it's very difficult to do so at the same time as focusing properly on what's being said. What people who raise this objection generally mean is that it's difficult to take notes at the same time as analysing the information and thinking about how to respond.

This is a phenomenon which I often see in meetings: the person being addressed adopts a listening posture (see "active listening" above) but as soon as the speaker has finished, the listener pays only lip-service to what was said ("OK . . .", "I hear what you say . . .", "I see where you're coming from . . .", "That's a good point . . .") and then takes the conversation off in a completely different direction, demonstrating conclusively that he or she HASN'T really listened. If writing down what the other person is saying prevents your brain from using the time to analyse and formulate your next response, so much the better. Your next response can only properly be formulated on the basis of what the other person has actually said and what you've therefore written down.

Taking notes of what is being said not only gives you richer raw material for constructing a response, but it will actually give you *more* time to think about your response. If you don't take notes, then you're probably looking the other person in the eye to demonstrate how attentively you're listening (or pretending to listen, including pretending to yourself) and because you're looking them in the eye, as soon as they stop talking you're obliged to jump in and respond. You can't keep looking them in the eye and say nothing because that will make both of you rather uncomfortable.

If, on the other hand, you're alternating between looking the other person in the eye and looking down at the page on which you're taking notes, then when they stop talking, you've got more time to look down at your notes and to formulate a response based on *what was actually said.*

(A practical hint: experiment with different writing implements to find one which allows you to take notes fastest. I'm most comfortable with a propelling pencil. Use an A5 note-book rather than A4 – or divide your A4 into two columns with a line down the middle of the page – so that your hand doesn't have to waste time moving back and forth across the whole page.)

Listening to Myself

As well as listening to the other person in a meeting, it's crucial also to *listen to yourself*. By this I don't mean listening to your own voice, but listening to your head, to what is now happening in your brain as a result of the words you've heard, to the thoughts and ideas which those words are now causing to be formed inside your skull. Those thoughts and ideas will also be influenced by the tone of voice that was used when the words were spoken – and by the facial expression which accompanied them (so use your *eyes* when you're listening as well as your ears and your hands). There are many different intonations, emphases and gestures which Jim might have used when he said: "It's very interesting but . . .". Some of them may have suggested genuine interest to you, or a total lack of interest, or you may have found it difficult to interpret the words one way or another.

Now that you've taken notes, perhaps you've underlined a few words because they're the ones which have triggered a thought or an idea in your mind:

> *"I've been looking at your documentation. It's very interesting, but at first glance, I think this is a little bit over-engineered for our needs. And officially all our budgets are frozen until the end of the year".*

Looking down at your notes, there are all sorts of things which could now be going on in your head as a result of Jim's words. There's ambiguity in there; there's stuff that Jim hasn't said clearly and stuff that he may be thinking but has left unsaid; there are elements on which you probably need more information; there are areas where perhaps you have a hypothesis as to what's going on but need confirmation; maybe there are possible solutions which you will need Jim's help to identify.

For example, looking at the first phrase you've underlined, "It's very interesting", you may be wondering what has led Jim to start with a positive, despite what follows next. Is he genuinely interested or is he just trying to soften the blow before saying no? Perhaps the way he said these words suggested to you that the door is still open – or perhaps that the door was being firmly slammed. Maybe you're telling yourself there's a paradox here which you need to resolve because on the one hand Jim is signalling interest in your product/service but then he seems to be finding excuses not to act.

Looking at "at first glance", perhaps you're wondering what Jim means by that; or perhaps you're telling yourself that he hasn't yet had a chance to read the documentation fully and that if he will only allow you to go through it with him in more detail, he may yet share your view that the product/service perfectly meets his requirements.

Looking at "a little bit" over-engineered, perhaps you're wondering what exactly Jim means by that. Does he think your product is 1 or 2 per cent over-engineered, or is he using understatement to soften the blow and actually thinks that it's at least 50 per cent over-engineered? Perhaps you're telling yourself that "a little bit" means it may not be difficult to close the gap and to provide something which exactly meets Jim's needs. Perhaps you disagree with Jim's assessment and want to be allowed to explain why. Perhaps you're wondering what would happen if you did agree to re-engineer and to close the gap. Perhaps you're wondering precisely what you'd need to do to resolve the over-engineering problem to Jim's satisfaction.

Looking at "officially all our budgets are frozen", perhaps you're asking yourself what has led Jim to add the word "officially", rather than just baldly stating "all our budgets are frozen". Perhaps, hearing the phrase "officially all our budgets are frozen", you're telling yourself that "unofficially" there's probably some leeway. Perhaps you're wondering exactly what you'd need to do so that "unofficially" some budget did become available.

Perhaps, looking at "until the end of the year", you're telling yourself that it sounds as if you can do a deal as soon as the new financial year opens.

Perhaps overall you're wondering what led Jim to call the meeting. If it's just to say no, he could quite easily have done that by email or over the phone. Perhaps you're telling yourself that since he DID call the meeting rather than sending an email or making a call, then, after all, this is the opening round in a negotiation.

These are just some of the things which might now be happening in your head as a result of the notes you took which allowed you to listen accurately to what Jim actually said in the meeting. And now that you've identified what's going on in your head, you're ready to respond.

Chapter Summary

- Listening, despite appearing deceptively easy, is difficult to do effectively because our emotions distort our view of what was actually said and because we're already busy analysing and for-mulating responses whilst the other person is still speaking.

- Rigorous listening involves disengaging your analytical faculties and engaging instead your writing hand, to note scrupulously what the other person says. Writing down what the other person says in his or her order, and using his or her words, helps to obviate the pernicious effects of emotion and analysis on listen-ing – and provides rich raw material which will greatly serve the productivity of the meeting.

- Rigorous listening also involves listening to yourself, to the thoughts and ideas which the other person's words – and the way in which they were said – generate in your head.

8

Responding: first principles

What you will have acquired by the end of the chapter:

A first level of awareness and understanding of three paths for responding in a meeting, each of which will always demonstrate to the other person that you have listened accurately to them and, more importantly, that you have done something with what you heard; which will help to get the unsaid said; and which will consistently help the meeting to advance.

Now that you've identified what's going on in your head, you're ready to respond . . .

And since you want to be clear, candid, direct and straight to the point in your response, to replace the implicit with the explicit, the unsaid with the said – and to encourage and enable the other person to do the same – that response will need to be completely consistent with what you've identified is now going on in your head.

But before looking at formulating your response as a function of the thoughts and ideas which the other person's words and gestures have generated inside your brain, let's take a moment to examine the consequences of doing otherwise.

I'll stick with the meeting example from the previous chapter. Jim, your client, has just told you: "It's very interesting, but at first glance, I think this is a little bit over-engineered for our needs".

Because of the inability of most people to listen effectively either to the other person or to themselves, the most likely responses to such a statement, in descending order of probability, are:

1. "Why do you think it's over-engineered, Jim?"
2. "But Jim, if you look at the specifications – here they are – you'll see that there's a very close fit with your needs. And here are

the test results which conclusively show that . . . And another thing . . ." (i.e. you'll just start getting your arguments out).

3. "That sucks, Jim! I think you're really missing an opportunity here".

What's going on with these responses and where are they likely to lead?

1. "Why Do You Think It's Over-Engineered, Jim?"

With this response, you're asking the other person to justify his or her position. You've also demonstrated that you haven't listened – or that despite your attempts to listen, you haven't heard what the other person actually said. Jim didn't say "it's over-engineered", he said "it's a little bit over-engineered". If you want Jim to justify his words, it will surely be much more fruitful from your standpoint to explore the words "a little bit" with him rather than to explore the words "over-engineered".

But even if Jim really had said "it's over-engineered", then "Why do you think it's over-engineered?" is still an unproductive question to ask. Regrettably it is probably the default reaction for most of us when we hear something which we didn't want to hear:

> **Him/her:** Unfortunately, we don't want to take this any further.
> **You:** *Why not?*

> **Him/her:** Before making a decision, I just want to shop around a bit and look at some alternatives.
> **You:** *Why do you want to do that?*

> **Him/her:** I don't agree with you.
> **You:** *Why not?*

> **Him/her:** I'm leaving you!
> **You:** *Why?*

101

There are a number of reasons why such responses are unproductive – or rather counter-productive. First of all, responding in this way is manipulative, albeit unconsciously manipulative rather than deliberately so. The reason for asking the question "Why do you want to shop around?" is most likely to be that you want the other person to make their decision WITHOUT shopping around. The reason for asking "Why are you leaving me?" is most likely to be that you want the other person to stay.

But in neither case have you actually said what you want. Your words are inconsistent with your thoughts. You're not asking the questions because you want to understand, objectively, the other person's reasons; you're asking the questions because you fully intend to try to shoot down in flames each of those reasons in the hope of getting the other person to change their mind. But you haven't acknowledged this.

Manipulation of this sort, or of any sort, is not good for the establishment of trust and confidence between you and the other person; but, even more importantly, it's also highly counter-productive in terms of achieving your ends. If you want someone to do something, inviting them to explain all of their reasons for doing exactly the opposite is unlikely to be helpful to you. Many training programmes, particularly in the area of sales, will claim to teach you how to "deal with objections". In our view, it's far more helpful to teach sales people not to generate objections in the first place. Questions like "Why is it over-engineered?" or "Why do you want to shop around before making a decision?" are guaranteed to provoke a tsunami of objections.

The more you invite someone to expose his or her arguments in favour of doing something (or not doing something) the more difficult it will be for them to go back on those arguments. You're painting them into a corner. You won't in any case gain by making them feel cornered, but you most especially won't gain by putting them into the particular corner where they will feel obliged to do the exact opposite of what you'd like them to do.

In addition, "Why?" or "Why not?" questions will give you absolutely no help in identifying whether there's room for negotiation. Consider the difference, at this and every other level, between the question "Why is it difficult?" and the question "What can I do to make it easier?"; or between "Why is it over-engineered?" and "What do I need to do, at the engineering level, to ensure that the fit is right?"

2. "But Jim, If You Look at the Specifications . . ."

With this kind of response, you're now the one doing the justifying. You haven't been asked to provide arguments and explanations, but nevertheless you're getting them out – and lots of them. This is much more likely to increase the effort you'll need to make to bring the other person round to your way of thinking. Arguments which you get out at your own initiative, without the other person's invitation or permission to do so, are unlikely to generate anything more helpful than counter-arguments. You've gone onto the attack – and the other person will instinctively go into defence mode and respond by picking off your arguments.

3. "That Sucks, Jim!"

With this kind of response, you've given in too easily, thrown in the towel at the very first setback. Whilst this may indeed be the end of the road for you in terms of making the sale, for the moment *nothing that Jim has actually said allows you legitimately to draw that conclusion.*

How might you react instead, in ways that are more productive both for the result of the meeting and for its impact on the relationship?

Responding Using What's Now Happening in Your Head

At the end of the last chapter, I suggested a number of different things which might be happening in your head as a result of having listened to Jim and which you had identified as a result of then listening to yourself. Being explicit with the other person about any one of those thoughts and ideas will be far more helpful in allowing the meeting to advance than the alternatives above. Here are a number of suggestions for ways in which you could make significant progress in the meeting by sharing those thoughts and ideas with Jim and, crucially, getting his reaction to them. I will show further along how all of these different suggestions adhere to a simple set of principles.

> **Jim:** *I've been looking at your documentation. It's very interesting, but at first glance, I think this is a little bit over-engineered for our needs. And officially all our budgets are frozen until the end of the year.*

> **You:** Jim, a lot of that doesn't sound very encouraging for me, but nevertheless you did start by saying: "It's very interesting". Tell me more about that.

Or

> **You:** Jim, despite everything else you went on to say, when I heard "It's very interesting", it gave me the impression that I shouldn't yet abandon all hope. How do you react to that?

Or

> **You:** Jim, on the one hand you've raised a number of possible obstacles, but you've also said that the documentation is "very interesting". Where do we go from here?

Or

> **You:** Jim, what leads you to talk about just a "first glance" of the documentation?

104

Or

You: Jim, based on your saying "<u>At first glance</u> I think this is a little bit over-engineered", I feel the need to spend 15 minutes going through the documentation with you in detail. How would you feel about that?

Or

You: Jim, hearing you say "<u>At first glance</u>" makes me want us to have a much more detailed second glance together . . .

Or

You: Jim, what exactly do you mean by "<u>a little bit</u> over-engineered?"

Or

You: Jim, hearing you say that you think this is "<u>a little bit</u> over-engineered", I'm telling myself that it shouldn't be difficult for us to close the gap.

Or

You: Jim, I have a different point of view regarding the engineering level and I'd like to take a few minutes to explain why. How do you feel about that?

Or

You: Jim, if we can re-engineer the product so that it exactly fits your needs, what could I hope for on your part?

Or

You: Jim, help me out here. How would I need to re-engineer the product so that it DOES fit your needs?

If, using responses like these, you have established that the "over-engineering" problem is not after all an insuperable one, you can also then use the same principles to clarify the apparent budget issue:

> **You:** Jim, what exactly do you mean when you say that all your budgets are frozen "<u>officially</u>"?

Or

> **You:** Jim, hearing you say that your budgets are frozen "<u>officially</u>", I'm telling myself that "<u>unofficially</u>" there may be some leeway . . .

Or

> **You:** Jim, what would I need to do so that perhaps "<u>unofficially</u>" some budget *does* become available?

Or

> **You:** Jim, hearing you say that your budgets are frozen "<u>until the end of the year</u>", I tell myself that I can perhaps look forward to inking a deal on January 2nd . . .

Or

> **You:** Jim, hearing you say that your budgets are frozen "<u>until the end of the year</u>", I'm thinking that if I can propose some flexibility on the payment terms, then perhaps we can still do a deal?

Perhaps you just want to clarify the apparent paradox between Jim's emphasis on the over-engineering and the budget constraints – and the fact that he's nevertheless invited you to a meeting:

> **You:** Jim, I'm wondering what led you to want a face-to-face meeting with me today, despite what you've just said about over-engineering and frozen budgets?

Or

You: Jim, I'm telling myself that if you wanted a face-to-face meeting with me today, despite what you've said about over-engineering and frozen budgets, then it's probably not yet time for me to throw in the towel. Well?

Deploying any of the responses above (and this list of suggestions is far from exhaustive) will *always* help the meeting to advance because things will immediately become clearer.

None of them will give you a guarantee of leaving the meeting having made a sale – but Jim's answers to your questions or invitations will necessarily and immediately allow you to identify whether or not the door is open. If it is shut, you will avoid beating on it fruitlessly, wasting your own time and his – and you will consequently leave the meeting at least with the esteem in which you are held by Jim intact and possibly enhanced. If the door is open, however small that opening may be, you can continue to apply the same principles to pursue the opportunity and to discover rapidly how best to seize it.

With each of the suggested responses, you will be doing one of three things. Either (i) you will be encouraging and enabling Jim to say what up until now he has left unsaid, to share with you explicitly what's actually happening in HIS head; or (ii) you will be telling Jim explicitly what's actually happening in YOUR head and getting his reaction to that; or (iii) you will be working with Jim to identify a solution or at least a next step.

These three possibilities are, like everything else in the book, the fruits of the research into effective verbal behaviour patterns in meetings and conversations carried out by my colleague, Philippe de Lapoyade. The crucial focus for him was on the constructs and responses which helped to produce results rapidly. As a result of his observations, Philippe identified that listening to the other person's words and then listening to the impact of those words on yourself opens up three possible paths in a dialogue which will always produce something to help the meeting advance:

1. Either I proceed from the other person and what's happening in his/her head (HIM/HER).
2. Or I proceed from myself and what's happening in my head (ME).
3. Or I proceed from myself and the other person at the same time to find a solution (HIM/HER + ME = US).

Each of these choices will allow you to demonstrate to the other person not just that you have heard what they have said but also that you have done something with what you have heard. You will use your time and energy more effectively, you will make more impact and you will be more comfortable.

Here are the principles which lie behind each of these three paths:

1. **HIM/HER**: Decoding the **other person's** words or actions
   This involves dealing with the **PAST**, usually the immediate past ("What did you mean by what you just said?", "How am I to interpret what you just did?") but sometimes the more distant past ("What led you to agree to see me today?"). It requires posing questions like the three just above or: "What are you trying to tell me when you say . . . ?", "What leads you to ask . . . ?", "What's your purpose in saying/doing . . . ?"; or it requires issuing invitations like: "Tell me more about . . .", "Go on . . ." or "Give me more detail".

2. **ME**: Expressing what's going on **in my own head**
   This involves dealing with the **PRESENT**, with what is actually happening in your own head at this moment in time. It requires telling the other person what, at this moment and as a result of what you've just heard or what you've just seen, you **THINK**,

you **WANT**, you **NEED** – and getting the other person's reaction to that. It requires statements such as "I want" ("I'd like"), "I need" or "Hearing you say ABC, I tell myself that XYZ" – and always following those statements with an invitation to the other person to respond to them.

3. **US (=HIM/HER + ME):** Identifying or defining **together with the other person** a **solution** or a next step, or getting a counterpart from them
This necessarily involves a **FUTURE** course of action. It requires posing questions like "What am I going to need to do so that you . . . ?", "What do you require from me so that . . . ?", "Where do we go from here?", "If I do X, what will you do in return?".

Table 8.1 shows a schematic way of looking at these three paths:

Table 8.1

Title	HIM/HER	ME	US (Him/ Her + Me)
Principles	I dig, decipher, I get more information, I find out what's really happening in HIS/HER head	I tell the other person what's really happening in MY head, what I think, what I want, what I need	I identify a solution with the other person, I launch an action, identify a next step
Applications	*"What do you mean by . . . ?"* *"What leads you to . . . ?"* *"Tell me more about . . ."*	*"Hearing you say . . . , I tell myself . . . What do you think?"* *"I want . . . (I'd like . . .) What do you think?"* *"I need . . . What do you think?"*	*"What do I need to do, so that you . . . ?"* *"If I . . . , what will you do . . . ?"* *"What do we do?"*

What Happens in YOUR Head Is Entirely Up to You

I don't want you to interpret any of the responses I proposed above as suggestions for what SHOULD be happening in your head as a result of listening to Jim's words. That's entirely up to you. What's important here is not the actual words which Jim uses but the impact which those words have on you. There's a hoary old joke which illustrates this distinction succinctly:

> **Q:** What's the difference between a lady and a diplomat?
> **A:** If a diplomat says, "Yes," he perhaps means "Perhaps".
> If a diplomat says, "Perhaps," he definitely means "No".
> If a diplomat says, "No", he's no diplomat.

On the other hand,

> If a lady says, "No", she perhaps means "Perhaps".
> If a lady says, "Perhaps", she definitely means "Yes".
> If a lady says, "Yes", she's no lady.

I don't endorse the old-fashioned sexism of the "joke", but it does demonstrate how exactly the same words can have an entirely different impact, depending on who says them.

You Don't Have to Be Right

If you choose to pursue the "ME" path in your initial exchange with Jim, the interpretation you put on his words may be entirely erroneous, but by explicitly sharing your hypothesis with the other person, you give him or her the opportunity to confirm or reject it, with immediate impact on the clarity of the exchange:

> **You:** Jim, hearing you say that your budgets are frozen "officially", I'm telling myself that "unofficially" there may be some leeway . . .

Jim: *Well when you're as long in the tooth as me, there are usually ways of getting round these things with a bit of creativity . . .*

Or alternatively

Jim: *No, I'm afraid there's no leeway at all. When I said "officially" I meant to emphasize that the decision comes from the CFO, the budgets are completely and irrevocably frozen until Jan 1 and I have no way of unfreezing them.*

What If You Didn't Hear the Other Person's Words Accurately?

You can only ever deal with what you've actually heard. Perhaps you've forgotten your notebook and pencil, perhaps, despite your best efforts to listen, you've only partially heard what the other person said, perhaps you've been unable to shake off your instinct to "focus on the facts" or to stop your emotions getting in the way – and perhaps therefore what you heard in the conversation with Jim was just "It's over-engineered for our needs". (Or perhaps this time that's what Jim really did say.)

Even if you haven't listened accurately and haven't heard everything the other person said, you are still able to listen to yourself, to the impact on you of those words that you DID hear. Identifying what's actually going on in your head and then sharing that explicitly with the other person will result in you being able to replace a potentially counter-productive response like:

"Why do you think it's over-engineered?"

with a far more productive one like:

"Well, Jim, I'm initially discouraged to hear you say that you think the product is over-engineered.(ME) I still very much

want us to be able to do a deal together.(ME) What do I need to do with the product at the engineering level for you to be comfortable about the fit with your needs?"(US)

It's almost certainly reflections like these in your head which led you in the first place to respond with "Why do you think it's over-engineered?" And what you're almost certainly looking ultimately to produce with the question: "Why do you think it's over-engineered?" is the answer to: "What do I need to do with the product at the engineering level for you to be comfortable about the fit with your needs?" *Slow down, listen to yourself and then think out loud.* Share your thought process with the other person. Invite him to work on "How to . . ." rather than "Why not to . . .".

If you DO still insist on finding out why Jim thinks the product is over-engineered (or why your teenager won't tidy his bedroom or why your husband doesn't like your favourite restaurant), then at least be clear what leads you to ask the question. Expose your thoughts to the other person *in the order in which they came to you*: "As I'm hoping that I can get you to change your mind about that Jim, I need to understand why you think the product is over-engineered".

Let's look at a couple more short examples of how using the three paths – HIM/HER, ME, US – in dialogue will help the meeting to advance by getting the unsaid stuff said. Both of these examples are inspired by my own recent experience.

"In theory . . ."

Not long ago, I ran a seminar at a business school in Paris. The seminar finished on Saturday afternoon. I had brought along my own video equipment and didn't fancy either lugging it home with me on the train or delaying my return to my family by taking the equipment back to our office on the other side of Paris. The most appealing solution appeared to be to leave the equipment on my client's premises until Monday morning when I could pick it up and return it to the office. I asked the girl at reception what she thought of me leaving the equipment in a cupboard until Monday. She reflected for a moment and then replied:

"In theory, that's not possible".

The knee-jerk reaction to a statement like this is often "Why not?" or "But it's going to be really difficult for me otherwise because . . .", or "That's a shame". As I showed earlier, none of these choices will produce concrete results rapidly. Instead, I considered the three paths: HIM/HER, ME, US.

Hearing the receptionist's words, I might perhaps have been wondering what had led her to say "in theory" in this context. In that case I could simply have asked her:

"What leads you to say that 'in theory, that's not possible'?"
(HIM/HER)

Secondly, I might already have had a hypothesis as to what led her to say "in theory", in which case I could have said:

"Hearing you say 'in theory, that's not possible', I get the impression that in practice it may be! What do you say to that?" (ME)

Thirdly, given that *"In theory, that's not possible"* is just a statement and not a position *("I can't do that"* is a position), I might have wanted to invite the receptionist to be more precise and to take a position:

"So what do we do today, in practice?" (US)

Any of these responses would have helped the conversation get rapidly to a concrete conclusion. In real life, I chose the last option above. The answer I got was: "Well if you promise to pick it up before

113

10am on Monday morning, I guess I can put it in the cupboard". Problem solved in less than 30 seconds.

Obviously, in this particular instance, I was fortunate in that the receptionist's response to my request was not a firm refusal, but one which suggested a possible opening. On another day, she might have used words which suggested a more categorical position: "That's just not possible".

I would still have had choices among the three paths which would have helped the meeting to advance.

For example:

> *"I'm sad to hear that. (ME) But I'd really like you to make an exception for me! (ME) What would I need to do for there to be any chance of that happening? (US)"*

Or

> *"That's really bad news for me. (ME) But I do really want to be able to leave my kit in Paris. (ME) What do we do? (US)"*

With either of these responses, I would be working with the receptionist on the solution rather than on the problem ("Why is it not possible?") Her answer might have been:

> *"Well if you absolutely promise, hand-on-heart, to pick it up by 10am on Monday, then I guess I could make an exception".*

Or it might still have been:

> *"I'm afraid there's really nothing I can do. It's absolutely forbidden to leave stuff over the weekend".*

In either case, I would immediately know whether or not the request was negotiable. If I'd asked "Why isn't it possible?", I could have spent the entire weekend listening to reasons why it wasn't possible and I STILL wouldn't know definitely whether there was any room for negotiation.

A cross-cultural example

I was talking recently to a senior partner in a law firm in London who has a particular interest in cross-cultural communication. We were discussing the British penchant for understatement and the confusion it can cause with other cultures. As an example, he mentioned that when a British boss tells a British subordinate "I was a little bit disappointed by what you said in the meeting this morning", the common cultural communication codes will probably result in the subordinate understanding that his boss is in fact absolutely livid about what was said in the meeting. A French subordinate on the other hand, not yet used to British communication codes, might reasonably suppose that there was a minor problem which he shouldn't worry about too much.

In all cases, whatever the cultural backgrounds of the parties, using the three paths will ensure that there are no misunderstandings and that solutions are found:

> **Boss:** I was a little bit disappointed by what you said in the meeting this morning.
>
> **British subordinate:** *I'm mortified to hear that because when I hear you say that you're a little bit disappointed, I tell myself that I screwed up big time.*
>
> **Boss:** Precisely . . .
>
> **British subordinate:** *What do I need to do to ensure I don't do it again?*

Or, changing the cultural context:

> **Boss:** I was a little bit disappointed by what you said in the meeting this morning.

115

French subordinate: *I'm sorry to hear that. But please tell me, as I'm new to working with Brits, what exactly do you mean by: 'a little bit disappointed?'* (HIM/HER)

Boss: Well not to put too fine a point on it, old boy, I was hopping mad!

French subordinate: *Oh! Now it's clear! And very worrying for me! What do I need to do to earn your forgiveness?* (US)

Things have indeed become clearer. The unsaid has been said and can now be dealt with. Alternatively perhaps the French subordinate might use ME instead of HIM/HER:

Boss: I was a little bit disappointed by what you said in the meeting this morning.

French subordinate: *I'm sorry to hear that. But hearing you say a little bit disappointed, I tell myself that there was a small faux-pas in an otherwise solid performance.* (ME)

Boss: Well you'd be wrong there, old boy!

French subordinate: *Oh! It now sounds to me as if I made a vraie merde!* (ME)

Boss: I couldn't have put it better myself . . .

French subordinate: *I'm very disturbed to hear that. So how can I avoid doing that in a meeting in the future?* (US)

In the next chapter, I will explore further the riches which can accrue in meetings and conversations from using the three paths and I will continue to demonstrate that they will ALWAYS help the meeting to advance.

Chapter Summary

- Responding in a meeting in a way which will produce results and keep the meeting on track towards delivering your desired final outcome requires listening rigorously to the other person's words and the impact of those words on you – and on then sharing those thoughts openly.

- Using one of three alternative paths will always help the meeting to advance in terms of clarity, understanding and productivity.

  ○ HIM/HER – finding out what's really going on in the other person's head by asking

  ○ ME – telling the other person what's really going on in my head and getting their reaction

  ○ US – finding a solution, launching an action

- Whilst using these paths will always be helpful, you don't need to try to use one every time you open your mouth. A few times in a meeting will suffice to greatly increase the levels of understanding and productivity.

9

The three paths:
1 "HIM/HER" and
2 "ME"

What you will have acquired by the end of the chapter:

A more detailed understanding of the first two of the three paths for responding, of their uses and applications and of the benefits they can bring in terms of comprehension, clarity and productivity.

L et's look in more detail at each of the three paths and the prin‐ciples which underline them. We'll look at each one in order – HIM/HER and ME in this chapter, US in the next one – and uncover more fully, via examples, the ways in which they can be applied in meetings and conversations to allow you consistently to "talk lean", to be candid (and concise) about what's going on in your head without being blunt – and to encourage and enable the other person to do so too.

1. HIM/HER: Proceeding from the Other Person

You have listened closely to the words of the person speaking to you. You have then listened to yourself and to the impact those words have had on you; and you feel that there is still stuff which is UNSAID and which you want to be SAID. There are three reasons why this could be:

i)   You HAVE understood what was said but you have NOT understood the other person's motive for saying it. You will uncover the motive with questions like: "What leads you to say . . . ?", "What's behind what you just said . . . ?", "What's your objective in telling me that . . . ?" (This is particularly useful for dealing with what I call "oblique" questions – questions whose meaning is clear but whose import is not. "What do you think of John's leadership on the project?", "How long have you been in your job now?", "How busy are you this weekend?", "Are you looking at me?", "Can you let me have Jane's contact details?". It is surely wise before answering such questions to say "Before answering your question, I'd like to know what leads you to ask it?") This construction can also be used to identify the meeting objective of someone who has not announced one (see below).

ii) You have NOT UNDERSTOOD what was said and you need further explanation. The terms the other person is using may be insufficiently precise – or perhaps they're using jargon or technical terms whose meaning you don't know. To get the explanation, you'll use questions like: "What do you mean by . . . ?", "Please explain to me . . .", "How am I to interpret . . . ?" (For example, "What do you mean by 'I have some reservations about the proposal'?"; "I need you to explain to me what you mean by 'exogenous growth theory'"; "How am I to interpret the lengthy hesitation before you said 'yes'?", "What did you mean by raising your eyebrows just now?")

iii) You HAVE understood what was said but feel that the information is incomplete and that you need more. To get the information, you'll use invitations like: "Tell me more about . . .", "Please go on", "I'm still listening . . .". (For example: "I want to talk about the order" – "Tell me more"; "Something's happened at the factory" – "I'm listening".)

The HIM/HER path is just as applicable to actions as it is to words as I hope some of the examples given above will have demonstrated ("What did you mean by raising your eyebrows just now?"). You may need to understand what has been the motivation behind someone's action or what someone means by an unspoken gesture. I will explore this theme – dealing with non-verbal communication – more fully in Chapter 11.

What's Your Objective?

In the example from Chapter 8 which featured Jim, the client, who thinks your product is probably a little bit over-engineered, I suggested as one possible response at the beginning of the meeting:

> *"Jim, I'm wondering what led you to want a face-to-face meeting with me today, despite what you've just said about over-engineering and frozen budgets?"*

Here, you are looking for the motivation of the other person behind an action. This is the obverse, the negative – in the photographic sense of the term – of "My objective is . . .".

It can always be very productive at the beginning of any meeting instigated by someone else to ask "What led you to ask for this meeting?"; or, if you've instigated a meeting with someone who is under no obligation to see you, to ask "What led you to agree to see me today?"

If someone comes into your office and launches into a speech involving long explanations and arguments – but they haven't yet told you what they want from you as a result of having given those explanations and arguments, you are quite entitled to invite them first to explain what their goal in coming to see you is:

> *"I'm happy to listen to your arguments and explanations. But FIRST, I need to know what you're expecting from me once I've done so".*

What the other person wants from you may be something which you're not prepared to grant whatever arguments you hear; or it may be something which you are prepared to grant without hearing any arguments at all. But you can't make that potentially time-saving judgement until you know what it is the other person is looking for. We have a client, the CEO of a €1bn company, who talks enthusiastically about the gains in productivity he has made as a result of practising the Interactifs Discipline. He tells us that he now listens politely to anyone on his staff who requests a meeting with him *for two minutes*. If in that time he hasn't yet heard the other person's meeting objective, he interrupts and says: "I can't listen properly to you until you have first told me clearly what you expect from me as a result of this meeting". On average he has halved the length of his meetings.

You don't have to be the boss to apply this principle, though the exact words you choose will depend on the nature of the relationship. If you've spent months chasing a prospective customer who obstinately seems to prefer doing business exclusively with your biggest competitor and she's finally agreed to see you, you may want as a priority at the beginning of the meeting to identify the prospect's motivation in finally accepting the meeting:

> **You:** We're both aware that at the moment you work exclusively with Smith's; and you undoubtedly know that if I've been chasing after a meeting with you for the last six months, it's with the hope of getting my hands on some of that business! So I hope I'm not being too bold if I ask you at the outset of the meeting: what led you to agree to see me today?

The customer's answer to this question (perhaps: "No particular reason, I just like to keep in touch with the market" or "Well, I think we're getting to a size where we should consider not putting all of our eggs into one basket" or "To be honest, we're feeling a bit let down by Smith's this week") will give you invaluable information and will clearly inform how you handle the rest of the meeting.

Because the Interactifs Discipline is emphatically exactly that, a "discipline" and not a "methodology", you have broad choices and you could equally well start this meeting on the "ME" path or on the "US" path:

You: Given that I've been hammering (not too insistently, I hope) on your door for the last six months, the fact that you've finally agreed to a meeting suggests to me either that I've completely worn you down or that I've got at least a sniff of an opportunity today! How do you react to that? (*ME*)

Or

You: I'm conscious that at the moment you work exclusively with Smith's and that I've consequently got something of a hill to climb if I'm to get listed. But tell me, what would I need to do to get at least part of the way up that hill today? (*US*)

2. ME: Proceeding from Yourself

I have already given several examples of how a phrase like "Hearing you say ABC, I tell myself that XYZ" (or alternatives like "Given what you said, I'm thinking that . . ." or "In light of your . . . , I'm saying to myself . . .") will allow you succinctly to tell the other person what impact their words have had on you – and to get their reaction to that.

This construction ("Hearing you say . . . , I tell myself . . .") is a far richer alternative to what you may have heard referred to as "reformulation". This – "reformulation" or "paraphrasing" – is often taught to people in business and presented as an act of listening.

"Reformulation" usually involves the use of a phrase like "If I understand correctly, you . . .". It is at best insufficient as an act of listening because it involves mere repetition (as I showed with the example of the helpline technician in Chapter 7). At worst, it can be used in a highly manipulative manner.

Let's look at how: "If I understand correctly, you . . ." is used and compare it to: "Hearing you say . . . , I tell myself that . . .".

> **Car showroom customer:** I'm interested in looking at your hatchback models.
>
> **Car salesman:** *So if I understand correctly, you've come in today to look at the hatchbacks?*

This is mere paraphrasing. No value has been added to the conversation, nothing has happened to take it forward. The salesman has heard the customer's words, but has done nothing at all with them. Alternatively, reformulation is sometimes used differently:

> **Car showroom customer:** I'm interested in looking at your hatchback models.
>
> **Car salesman:** *So if I understand correctly, you've come in today to buy a hatchback?*

You can see what's going on here – and it ain't pretty! The customer's words have indeed been reformulated by the salesman – but twisted into a form which better suits his purpose. If the customer notices what's happened, and he probably will, he's going to start the meeting thinking: "I'm going to have to watch this one. Give him an inch and he'll take a mile". This is the precise opposite of the trust and confidence which should inform a successful meeting from the start.

Compare that with any of the following alternatives where "If I understand you correctly, you . . ." is replaced by "Hearing you say . . . , I tell myself . . .".

> **Car showroom customer:** I'm interested in looking at your hatchback models.
>
> **Car salesman:** *Hearing you say that, I tell myself that I can already dispense with a large chunk of the sales manual called "Discovering the customer's needs"!* (ME)

The crucial difference between "Hearing *you* say . . . , *I* tell myself . . ." and "If *I* understand correctly, *you* . . ." is that someone who uses the former has demonstrated not only that they've heard what has been said *but also that they've done something with it.*

Or

> **Car showroom customer:** I'm interested in looking at your hatchback models.
>
> **Car salesman:** *OK. And whilst I take you over there, I'd like you to tell me more about your project so that I can best adapt my presentation to your specific interests.* (HIM/HER)

Or

> **Car salesman:** *And I'd be very happy to show them to you! And if I find you one that ticks all the right boxes, what are you planning to do today?* (US)

There were two other elements which appeared in the "ME" column in Table 8.1, two other things which might be going on in your head as a result of listening to the other person and which you can productively share with him or her: the expression of an ambition ("I want") or the expression of a requirement ("I need").

I Want/I Need

"I" is a word of extraordinary power but one from which too many people shy away, often at considerable cost to the impact they make. In business, people often hide behind "we" ("we at the bank" or "we at Smith's"). Obviously your customers have a relationship with your company – if you leave the company it's not certain all of your customers will follow you – but they also have a relationship with you, and it is successful personal relationships which lead to business being won or retained. It is much more powerful and seductive to say to a potential customer: "I really want to work with you" than to say "We're hoping we can possibly reach a mutually beneficial agreement".

People also tend to hide behind impersonal statements like "That's unacceptable" or "That's rubbish" or even "That's fabulous". It's always more powerful and better for the relationship (and more legitimate – see Chapter 7) to personalize the statement, to favour the first person over the second or the third: "I can't accept that" or "I'm disappointed with that piece of work" or "I really love that idea".

It is ALWAYS legitimate to tell someone with whom you work, whether they're a client or a colleague and whatever your respective levels within the hierarchy, what you want from them or need from them. Obviously how you feel about telling the other person what you want or need from them will depend on your relationship. Some people would find it a lot easier to ask a subordinate to come in and work at the weekend than to ask their boss to do so; for others, the precise opposite would be true. But in all cases, if you're uncomfortable telling someone what you want or need from them, then just say so.

> **Boss to subordinate:** I'm uncomfortable imposing on my team in what should be their free time, but I'm afraid I want you to come in on Saturday morning to help with the presentation.

Equal-to-Equal

When people WANT something or NEED something, they very often replace the straightforward "I want" or "I need" with a much less direct question: "Would it be all right if I just went through my presentation?", "Would it be OK to meet up next week?", "Would you mind making the payment of the invoice this week?", "Can I go to the bathroom please, Miss?"

These formulae, whilst polite, lack transparency, impact and often clarity. There is inconsistency between what's happening in your head ("I want us to have another meeting next week") and what's coming out of your mouth ("Would it be OK to meet up next week?") Is going to the bathroom negotiable? Probably not! Why not therefore be clear about that: "I need to go to the bathroom Miss!"?

In particular, these formulae establish an unequal relative hierarchy. They are usually submissive, but sometimes arrogant if used ironically ("If you can spare the time from organizing your busy social life, would you mind stepping into my office?"). They are never "equal-to-equal". By asking permission for something (without irony), you are adopting the position of a supplicant. Whatever the actual relative hierarchy, *as long as you always speak with politeness and courtesy*, then you will always generate more respect and create a more successful relationship if you present yourself as someone who is persuaded that they have an equal right to be on the planet. Your client or your boss will have greater respect for someone who has the courage of their convictions, who is ready to take a position and defend it, than for someone who presents themselves as a willing serf ready to execute any order without analysis or opinion.

This principle of communicating on an equal-to-equal basis applies just as strongly when you're talking to people below you in the food chain. You will have more successful relationships if you avoid arrogance just as much as if you avoid submissiveness. Your suppliers, your subordinates – and the people who come to clean your office in the evening – have the same right to be on the planet as you do and you should address them on an equal-to-equal basis. This simply means being clear, direct and straight to the point as well as being polite and courteous. Just as in the other direction, you will generate greater respect.

So please make the following translations:

> *"Would it be all right if I just went through my presentation?"* → *"At this point in the meeting, I want to go through my presentation. How do you feel about that?"*
>
> *"Would it be OK to meet up next week?"* → *"I want to meet up next week. How would that be for you?"*
>
> *"Would you mind making the payment this week?"* → *"I need you to make the payment this week".*

"Perhaps you'd like to take the car for a test drive?" → *"At this stage in our exchange, I recommend we take the car out on the road so you can get a feel for its performance. What do you think?"*

"Do you ever actually use that vacuum cleaner?" → *"I'd like you to run the vacuum under my desk this evening please".*

Equal-to-Equal in Your Personal Life: Elegance Is an Attitude

It's not just your business relationships which will benefit from an increased dose of "equal-to-equal".

Sometimes in a seminar people have asked us "Can this approach be used with members of the opposite sex?" (OK, it's mostly men who've asked this!) To which the answer is: this is an approach based on openness and transparency for dealing more effectively with other members of the human race – and the opposite sex, whatever that happens to be, is composed entirely of members of the human race!

Seduction in your business life and seduction in your personal life have this much in common: you will only be successful if you create trust and confidence and behave in an attractive and appealing manner. As I hope I made clear in the introductory chapter, the approach described in these pages is not a "technique" or a "methodology" which will be effective if *applied* to members of the opposite sex. It is a "*discipline*" which you *apply to yourself* – and then hopefully YOU will be effective with other people, of whatever gender.

Philippe de Lapoyade tells an anecdote about this which delights me. Once in a seminar in which the participants were exclusively young, single and male, one of them asked him the question above: "Does this work on girls?" After having corrected the apparent misconception that the Interactifs Discipline is an approach which "works" on other people, Philippe asked the young man what had led him to ask the question. He replied that he was wondering if any of the tools he'd just discovered could be used to start a conversation with a girl in, say, a nightclub. Philippe asked the young man to describe what happened when he went out to a club.

"Well", he replied, "I go out with my mates. We have a few drinks at the bar, we have a look round and with a bit of luck I see someone who looks attractive and unattached. I have another drink to get my courage up and eventually I go over to try to start a conversation". "So far so good" said Philippe, "what do you say?"

"It varies, but it's usually something like 'Would you like to have a dance?', 'Have I seen you before somewhere?', 'Are you waiting for someone?'" Doubtless there have been instances throughout the history of the human race where lines like these HAVE resulted in a dance being danced – and perhaps more! But equally doubtlessly, there are many more instances where they haven't.

Questions like those suggested above give the other person only two possible choices of response: "Yes!" or "No!" Given the limited choice available, the most likely response is the one which is most comfortable for the other person. The easiest – and therefore the most common – answer to the question "Would you like to have a dance?" is probably "No thanks". For the same reasons, the most likely response in a shop or a car showroom to the question "Can I help you?" is "No thanks, I'm just looking". (I am certain that this particular exchange happens millions of times a day, in hundreds of different languages, right across the planet.)

A "No thanks" doesn't necessarily kill the exchange stone dead, but the fact that it has started with a rejection certainly makes things more complicated and less comfortable.

"Would you like to have a dance?" is also submissive. You are asking permission and placing yourself in an inferior position.

"Let's start again," said Philippe. "What leads you to want to go up to a girl in a nightclub and say 'Would you like to have a dance?'" After Philippe had dealt with answers which showed up the limits of the analogy between personal seduction and business seduction (because in personal seduction the "unsaid" is part of the game), he eventually got the simple answer he was looking for.

"Well, I ask a girl if she'd like to dance because I want to have a dance with her!" "Try saying that!" said Philippe.

"I'd really like to dance with you . . ." is always going to be more powerful, more appealing, more attractive and more seductive than "Would you like to have a dance?", just as "I'd like to have a drink with you" will always be more appealing than "Could I buy you a drink?"

I'll get back to social intercourse in nightclubs in a minute (there's certainly a whole book to be written on that subject alone) but first I want to demonstrate that the analogy is relevant to the business world. If, for example, you're buying a car and haven't yet decided on financing, I am persuaded that you are more likely to be seduced by a salesman who says "I really want you to arrange your financing through me" than by one who says: "Could I tell you about our financing deals?".

Let's go back to the club: behaving in an appealing manner, being candid but also courteous, involves saying what's really going on in your head, on being transparent, on thinking out loud. The young man in the nightclub could therefore simply inspire trust and confidence by sharing with the young lady his entire thought process.

"Hi. I was having a drink at the bar with some friends and I saw you standing over here; so I had another drink to get

my courage up and I've come over to say that I want to dance
with you. How do you find the idea?"

If all you can think of for introducing yourself is a really tired and
cheesy old chat-up line ("Have you got a map because I'm lost in your
eyes?" for example) then by all means use it – just be explicit about
what has led you to come up and try it out:

> *"Hi, look . . . um . . . I really want to talk to you and the only*
> *thing I've been able to come up with to start a conversation*
> *is a terribly cheesy old chat-up line. So here it is . . . 'Have*
> *you got a map because I'm lost in your eyes?' What did you*
> *think of it?"*
> *"You're right, it was rubbish!"*
> *"So what do we do now?"*

You are being open and transparent and you are presenting yourself
on an entirely equal-to-equal footing. After that it really doesn't
matter how tired and cheesy the line is – it's no longer the point.

If on the other hand you just sidle up and whisper "Hi. You're hot!
Do you have a map, because I'm lost in your eyes?" you are behaving
as a seducer, which is NOT the same as behaving seductively. You are
attributing to yourself a position of superiority and consequently
acting with condescension.

Philippe's anecdote continues with an exploration of what happens
after the initial dance. He asked his curious participant how he moved
things on once he was on the dance floor.

"Well", answered the participant, "if things seem to be going well, I
might shuffle a little closer to see if there's any resistance. If there
isn't, then I move closer still".

"I have a different suggestion", said Philippe, "next time, instead of
moving closer, move a bit further away. And then TELL the young
lady that you want HER to come closer to you".

Philippe claims that at the end of the first day of this particular seminar, he invited the participants to go out in the evening with half of the group applying what they'd just learnt and the other half, for control purposes, applying a more traditional approach ("Would you like to have a dance?").

"NO COMPARISON!" they all chorused the next day!

Chapter Summary

- The HIM/HER tools will help when you HAVE understood what was said but not why it was said; when you have NOT understood what has been said; or when you HAVE understood but need more information.

- The first ME tool ("Hearing you say . . . , I tell myself . . .") provides a much richer and safer alternative to "reformulation" because it allows you to demonstrate that you have processed information, rather than twisting it (via manipulation) or simply repeating it, parrot-fashion.

- The other two ME tools ("I want . . .", "I need . . .") allow you consistently to deal with other people on an equal-to-equal footing, to generate respect, to make impact . . . and to create clarity about your wants and needs.

10

The three paths:
3 "US"

What you will have acquired by the end of the chapter:

A more detailed understanding of the last of the three paths for responding; its uses and applications and the benefits it can bring in terms of comprehension, clarity and productivity.

3. US: Proceeding from the Other Person and Myself Together

We saw in Chapter 8 how the "US" path involved defining, together with the other person, a **future** course of action, finding a solution or launching an action.

There's an important general principle when it comes to solving problems which will save you a lot of time in meetings. This is that in any situation when you're trying to get something from someone else, it's THE OTHER PERSON WHO HAS THE SOLUTION. It's not you who best knows what it will take for you to get what you want, it's them. So just ask!

In simple situations, with little at stake, we do this instinctively. Imagine you're going to visit your brother who's just moved to Paris. You're taking the Eurostar to the Gare du Nord and then you need to find your way to your brother's apartment using public transport.

You call up your brother before leaving London to talk about getting to the apartment. It's unlikely that you'll start by giving him all of your ideas about how to get there: "Should I take the metro? What do you think of me taking line 4? No? Well what about line 5 then? Going north or south? Should I get off after six stops? Perhaps after three then? And what about turning left when I leave the metro station? No? Then what about right? Oh, I see, straight on. Should I walk about 100 metres?"

This would clearly be an inefficient way of getting the solution. You're not the one with the information – your brother is. You're much more likely simply to say, "I want to get to your place from the Gare du Nord on public transport. What do I need to do?" And your brother will give you very precise directions.

Unfortunately, in business situations, we usually make life more complicated for ourselves. The person doing the asking starts giving the other person all his or her own ideas, rather than just asking them for directions:

> *"Can we get the contract signed by next week? What if I offered a discount for rapid signature? I can fly someone over to pick it up. Maybe I can agree to accept the 90-day payment terms after all"*.

You clearly know how to ask for directions and probably do so frequently: "How do I get to Trafalgar Square?" There's every reason to use the exact same construct in meetings, when you have a clear target and just need to know how to get there. "How can I be sure of getting the final contract signed by next Friday?"

"If I . . . , What Will You Do?"
The obverse of:

> *"What do I need to do so that you . . ."*

is

> *"If I . . . , what will you do?"*

137

(Or "If on my side I . . . , what can I hope for on your side?", "Supposing that I . . . , what would you be tempted to do?", "In return for me . . . , what can I expect from you?" or any other similar construction.)

This option will allow you to get a counterpart from the other person and is indispensable in negotiations, since you don't want to give anything away without getting something in return.

> **Client:** Can you give me a 5 per cent discount?
>
> **Supplier:** *Yes. But if I do so, what can I expect from you in return?*

Or (an alternative way of phrasing the same demand):

> **Supplier:** *Yes. But first I need to know what I can hope for in return.*

You can also be specific about what sort of counterpart you're looking for:

> **Client:** Can you give me a 5 per cent discount?
>
> **Supplier:** *Yes. But if I give you the discount, what can I expect from you in terms of volume guarantees?*

Or

> **Supplier:** *Yes. But if I do so, what will you be able to do in terms of getting the contract signed rapidly?*

This is NOT the same as saying "If I give you a discount, will you sign the contract today?" It's not the same because:

1 Asking the other person a question which they have complete freedom to answer as they see fit is more respectful than giving them a binary choice.
2 You will get a richer, more informative response if you give the other person complete freedom to answer as they choose.

3 If the other person IS happy to sign the contract today, then in my view, despite the obsession in sales courses with the word "Yes", it will be more engaging for the other person and more satisfying for you if the words which come out of their mouth are "If we can agree on a discount, I'd be happy to sign the contract today" rather than "Yes, OK".

There are of course other ways of responding to "Can you give me a discount?" using the HIM/HER or ME paths. There's always a choice. For example:

Client: Can you give me a discount?

Supplier: *Yes I can. And I'm happy to hear that question because I tell myself that as long as we end up agreeing on the price, then the deal is done.* (ME)

Or

Client: Can you give me a discount?

Supplier: *No I'm afraid I can't. What else can I do to ensure that the deal still goes through despite that?* (US)

"What Do We Do?"

Behind this everyday phrase (which can be expressed in many different ways: "What now?", "Where do we go from here?", "And now what?", "What's the next step?", "How do we proceed from here?") lies a principle which can have a huge impact on the productivity of your meetings.

The principle behind this simple construct is that it invites the other person to TAKE A POSITION or MAKE A PROPOSAL. One of the reasons why meetings can drag on so very long and produce so very little is that participants don't take positions and other participants don't invite them to do so.

Let's look at two particular circumstances in which "What do we do?" will help the meeting or conversation to advance quickly.

1 Unblocking a situation

"What do we do?" invites the other person to suggest their solution when there are seemingly intransigent and opposing positions.

> *"On the one hand, I have a faxed confirmation of my reservation. On the other, the booking doesn't seem to be in the system. What do we do?"*
>
> *"You're telling me you really like the product but need me to reduce the price by 10 per cent. I'm telling you the maximum discount I can offer is 5 per cent. How can we move forward despite this gap?"*

Using "What do we do?" will help you quickly to work towards a common solution. In response to the second question above, there's clearly a difference in position between the customer who responds: "Well, if you can't reduce the price by 10 per cent then I'll have to find another supplier" and the one who responds "Well, if you can't reduce the price by 10 per cent, then we're going to have to look at the payment terms".

2 Giving your arguments the chance to produce something

It's all very well having thought up powerful and persuasive arguments before your meeting, but you need to ensure that you use them effectively and that they actually produce something. I have already suggested a first important principle in the deployment of arguments, which is to hold off giving them until the other person has invited you to do so. Only then will he or she be willing to listen with an open mind, rather than simply inventing counter-arguments.

A second principle is to state your position clearly first, before you start giving all of the arguments which underpin that position.

Most of us have a tendency, instilled in us at an early age, to argue deductively. We present our arguments, often a long list of them, before deducing "that therefore . . .". It is more efficient, more courteous, better for the relationship, to give the "conclusion" first. This is closely related to the principle (exposed in Chapters 3, 4 and 5) of stating your objective before giving the arguments which support the objective. If you get your arguments out before giving your position (or stating your objective), then either the other person will guess what your position is and be distrustful, or not guess and be wary.

With reference to the example at the start of Chapter 1 of a management consultant who wants to charge an additional fee AFTER some work has been done, compare and contrast these two approaches:

> **You:** I'm afraid the analyses turned out to be more complex than they initially appeared. We had to assign two more associates, it took up more management time as well as more travel time. There were unforeseen . . . (*and so on for several more minutes*) and regrettably we therefore want to increase the fee.

Versus

> **You:** I'm uncomfortable asking this after the fact rather than before, but I want to charge an additional fee for the extra analyses we carried out. I'm happy to explain why I think this request is legitimate . . . and I hope that we'll be able to agree on an amount.

A third principle (which I will revisit in more detail in the next chapter) is to deploy your arguments one at a time and to get the other person's reaction to each argument. Only by doing that will you be able to measure what impact each argument is having in terms of helping you to reach your announced objective. Then once the other person has reacted positively to one of your arguments, "What do we do?" will allow the argument to produce a concrete result by inviting the other person to take a position.

Imagine that you're advising a client on a foreign acquisition. You've done extensive due diligence, you've negotiated what you're confident is a fair price, the contract is drawn up and ready, but your client doesn't seem to be in any hurry to sign. For various reasons, you think it's important that the contract is signed this week:

- You've been watching the foreign exchange markets and you think the exchange rate is about to move against you.

- There are some significant tax benefits to making the deal before the end of this month.

- The seller has strong emotional ties to his business and you're worried that any delay might give him an excuse to change his mind and pull out.

- Some much bigger companies in your client's sector are due to report their results next week and you feel that your client's acquisition will get much less prominent coverage in the press than this week.

You call your client, David, and using the principles for opening meetings established in Chapters 3, 4 and 5, you say something like:

> *"Hi David. I'm conscious that I'm going to be asking for a big effort on your part. I can explain why my position has evolved – and I'm phoning you because I need us to agree on a firm time before the end of the week to ink the contract. What do you think?"*

The rest of the conversation may go like this:

> **David:** Well, I've got a lot of other critical stuff on and I'm sure a few more days won't make any difference.
> **You:** *I disagree. I think they may make a lot of difference.*
> **David:** Why?

> **You:** *Well, the first thing is we're expecting some exchange rate movement next week which could result in an increase in the cost of the acquisition in sterling equivalent.*
>
> **David:** That would be a problem for us.
>
> **You:** *So what do we do?*
>
> **David:** Can we get together with the seller on Friday at 2 pm?

What's happened here is that a "What do we do?" has allowed your first argument to produce a concrete result, without you even having to place the other three arguments.

Initially you have not given any arguments at all before first telling your client what you hope to achieve as a result of deploying those arguments. Having heard what you want, he has then invited you to share the arguments. You have not piled them up one after another, but have exposed only your first argument and asked the client to react to that. His reaction ("That would be a problem for us") indicated that he saw the merit of the argument. So you then simply used "What do we do?" to invite him to take a position.

I will say more about the principle of expressing yourself one idea at a time in Chapter 12.

Opening Your Meeting

The "US" tools can also be used for opening your meeting, either as part of the structure exposed in Chapter 5, or as an alternative to it.

The US question which will allow you to get the other person's specifications: "What do I need to do so that you . . . ?" (or "What do you need from me in order for you to . . .", or "What would need to happen on my side for there to be a chance that you . . ." or any similar formula) is a possible choice for the OBJECTIVE of your meeting. Some of the suggested meeting openings from Chapter 3 used this approach. For example, one of the suggested objectives for the financial advisor seeing a prospect was "What I'm looking for from today's meeting is to leave here with a clear understanding of what I and my colleagues at XYZ Bank need to do to have a chance of getting a mandate to manage your wealth, just as we do for Mr Smith".

Other examples of meeting openings from Chapter 3 also showed how US tools can be used to start your meeting as an alternative to the "way-in" structure explained in Chapter 5:

> *"John, how can I be sure that I can count on your punctuality in the future without it leading to a confrontation between us?"*

> *"John, I'm determined to resolve this issue once and for all even if I'm conscious of taking a hard line. I have decided that your punctuality at meetings is no longer negotiable. Now that you know that, what do we do?"*

> *"Peter, what can I do next quarter to get a raise to match Jane's without this request being a career-limiting move for me?"*

Further options for using US tools to start the same meetings include:

> *"John, what do I need to do so that this is the last time we ever have to discuss your time-keeping?"*

> *"John, about your time-keeping – what are we going to do?"*

> *"Peter, you gave Jane a raise and not me – but I feel I have at least as strong a case as she does. So what do we do?"*

Tying up the Loose Ends

Now that you have a thorough understanding of the rich array of options which the three paths give you and how these will always help your meeting to advance, let's use them to resolve unresolved issues from earlier in the book.

For example, in my opening paragraph to Chapter 6 (and elsewhere) I entertained the possibility that, despite your best efforts in introducing your meeting, the other person may not be receptive to your objective and may just say no. I have argued that if the answer really is no, it's better for you to discover this at the beginning of the meeting and avoid wasting time and perhaps poisoning the relationship by arguing fruitlessly. This is one of the many benefits of being clear about your intentions right at the start of the meeting.

But if your objective is met with an immediate "no", you have one last opportunity, created by the structure of your opening, before accepting that your time will more usefully be spent elsewhere:

> **You:** Jack, I really hope today that we can agree on a new way of working together which I'm happier with and which you feel able to accept . . . How do you feel about that?
>
> **Jack:** *You're wasting your time. I'm not changing anything.*
>
> **You:** Hmm! Well, I'm obviously disappointed that the meeting has started like this – and perhaps finished! But I'd like you to hear me out before taking such a firm position.

Or perhaps

> **You:** Well that certainly feels like a kick in the teeth. But now you know that I'd like some things to change in the way we work together, what do we do?

In terms of tying up loose ends, you may also have noticed that I haven't yet addressed all of the different situations which I used as examples at the start of Chapter 1 to give you a feel for the scope of the book.

145

I've used four of the situations (the latecomer, the burnt-down production line, the new boss and the management consultant) to provide illumination in Chapters 3, 4, 5 and 10, respectively, but I haven't yet addressed the opportunity which suddenly arises at a conference to talk to a prospect, the rude customer or the 2am taxi call.

I am confident that having got to this stage in the book, you now have plenty of ideas yourself for dealing effectively with these situations. Go back to the beginning of the book, think about different ways in which you could deal with each situation using the three paths – and then compare your suggestions with mine below.

The Prospect at a Conference

You: Hello. I'm John Smith from Acme Corp. Seeing you suddenly on your own, I tell myself that I've got a golden opportunity to speak to you for two minutes and I'll never forgive myself if I let it go. So what do you say? (*ME*)

Or

You: Hello, I'm John Smith from Acme Corp. How can I take advantage of the situation to grab your attention for two minutes without it being seen as too opportunistic? (*US*)

Or

You: Hello, I'm John Smith from Acme Corp. I've been hoping to speak to you for a few months now and suddenly I'm standing next to you and you're on your own. What do we do now? (*US*)

The Rude Client on the Phone

Client (shouting down the phone): *This is unacceptable! You're a bunch of incompetents!*

You: I don't like the turn this conversation is taking and I want us to advance without going down that route. What do you say? (*ME*)

Or

You: I'm absolutely ready to try to sort this out for you, but I do need you to be nicer to me. (*ME*)

Or

You: I'm going to find it much easier to sort this out if I'm not shouted at. So what do we do? (*US*)

The 2am Taxi

Attractive member of the opposite sex: *I suppose I ought to be thinking about getting a taxi.*

You: Well I suppose *I* ought to be thinking about asking you to stay! (*ME*)

Or

You: When I hear you say that you <u>suppose</u> you <u>ought</u> to be <u>thinking</u> about getting a taxi, I tell myself that it seems to be your head speaking and not your heart. (*ME*)

Or

You: What would I need to do for you to decide NOT to get a taxi? (*US*)

Or

You: How can I ask you, in a way which leaves you quite comfortable to say no if that's what you choose, to stay here instead of getting a taxi? (*US*)

And finally . . .

It was after coming across the three paths that I realized why the young man in the London Underground who so excited my admiration in Chapter 1 had been able to be so effective in his approach. If you look back at the example, you will now see why too.

Chapter Summary

- The US tools allow you rapidly to identify a solution or at least a next step. They will allow you to determine the other person's specifications for solving the problem, to agree on a counterpart, to unblock apparently intransigent positions and to help arguments produce something more helpful than mere counter-arguments.

11

Dealing with the non-verbal

What you will have acquired by the end of the chapter:

An appreciation of the scope and limitations of using and interpreting non-verbal communication; ideas on how to put your existing skills in this area (whether innate or acquired) at the service of more efficient exchanges and more successful relationships; and an understanding of how the tools for bringing clarity to spoken communication can be used just as effectively to bring clarity to unspoken communication.

Ever since Charles Darwin published *The Expression of the Emotions in Man and Animals* in 1872, the uses and meanings of non-verbal communication have exercised an abiding fascination for us. A measure of this is that in Darwin's lifetime the book was a bigger seller than *On the Origin of Species*. Interest has developed exponentially and over the last 60 years a whole new science has emerged – "kinesics" – devoted to the study and interpretation of body language.

Interactifs has no pretensions to expertise in this area. We are happy to leave it to others to offer advice on what may or may not be happening in the other person's head if they're scratching their nose, pursing their lips or crossing their legs. Our field – and my subject in *this* book – is VERBAL communication. But one of my recurrent themes is the preponderance in meetings and conversations of the "unsaid" and the extent to which this adversely affects the production of results and the enhancement of relationships. I therefore feel legitimate in including a chapter on the subject; but I will not be advising you on how to interpret the non-verbal elements in meetings and conversations. Instead I will make suggestions about what to do VERBALLY with your interpretations once you've made them. It's our view that what you do with your interpretation of the other person's unspoken communication will be far more significant for the efficiency of your exchanges and for the establishment, maintenance and enhancement of your relationships than whether your interpretation happens to be correct or not.

Our focus at Interactifs on the spoken has not made us blind to the importance of the unspoken. Non-verbal communication unquestionably plays a huge role in the way human beings interact with each other. Some of the most eloquent and powerful ways we have of communicating with other members of our species are unspoken: the warm smile, the gentle touch, the lingering glance, the dark frown, the bitter tears. Whilst there's no consensus on exactly how important such non-verbal elements are in exchanges between humans, estimates from different sources put it at anywhere between 57% and 93%. I'm sceptical about the precision of such numbers, but I'm persuaded by the broad conclusion that a very significant proportion of the communication going on when two or more humans are gathered together is non-verbal.

People have always – well before Darwin and well before kinesics – tried both to interpret the body language of others and to communicate through their own. Both of these skills are primarily innate and unconscious; but both have always taken place at a conscious level too. After all, before we developed speech, we had no choice but to try consciously to communicate without it.

But the proliferation of studies, books and courses on body language in recent years has made the desire consciously to interpret other people's non-verbal communication far more prevalent. And it's a short step from speculating about what might be going on in someone else's head as a result of their non-verbal communication to using your own body language to try to convey unspoken messages to others. It probably took about five minutes after a body language expert had first published the observation that looking to the left with your eyes is more often associated with the retrieval of facts and looking to the right more often associated with creation and fabrication for the first politician or businessman to deliberately look to the left when next telling a particularly whopping lie.

Kinesics, as capable and principled practitioners will happily acknowledge, is not an exact science. It deals with probabilities and not with certainties, with correlation and association rather than with causality. Rapid head-nodding does not always indicate impatience, just as impatience will not always be signalled by rapid head-nodding. As a result, the conscious but unacknowledged application of "body language skills" can often lead to complex and inefficient games of second-guessing: "He's adopted posture A, which means he's probably thinking B and therefore I should say/do C", or "If I adopt posture X, then she's probably going to think Y and therefore she'll say/do Z".

The advice below on replacing complexity and inefficiency with simplicity and effectiveness when dealing with other people's non-verbal communication, and with your own, is consistent with all of the principles for "talking lean" advanced throughout the book.

1. Dealing with Other People's Non-verbal Communication

The capable and principled body language experts referred to above will always recommend that no single body language signal should be used as a reliable indicator; and that understanding body language involves the interpretation of several consistent and simultaneous signals to support a particular conclusion.

I want to go further and suggest that NO conclusion about what's going on in the other person's head should be reached on the basis of non-verbal communication alone.

Hypotheses, Not Conclusions

We all have innate abilities for interpreting non-verbal communication which are present from birth and honed through experience and feedback as we grow up; and we may have added to those innate abilities through reading specialist books or attending specialist courses. But while the conscious observation and interpretation of several consistent and simultaneous non-verbal signals is a skill which can probably be acquired with years of study and practice, it cannot be acquired as a result of a short course in an agreeable off-site location. You may learn many useful and enriching things on a two-day body language course, but I am confident that you will not learn enough to know with absolute certainty what is really going on in another person's head as a result of their gestures, postures or expressions.

Sometimes, either instinctively or as a result of something you've learnt, you may have an idea about what the other person is thinking or feeling – but it's just that: an idea. If you have a PhD in kinesics, your hypothesis may be more informed – but it's still a hypothesis. At other times, you may be certain that the other person's body language is signifying something, but you will be completely unable to form a hypothesis as to what that something is.

In both cases, the relationship will best be served by sharing overtly with the other person what's now going on in YOUR head. If you're closely analysing the other person's posture, gestures and expressions and forming hypotheses about what they're thinking or feeling, you should let them know what you're doing. (If you have a PhD in kinesics, you should definitely let them know about THAT!) If you've observed some signals which you think are meaningful but haven't been able to form a hypothesis, just ask. You wouldn't be comfortable having your body language observed and analysed covertly by someone else, so don't do it to them.

Your interpretation of the other person's non-verbal signals may be entirely wrong, but that doesn't really matter. You will only start serving both the relationship and the efficiency of the meeting at the moment when you articulate your hypothesis and invite the other person to react to it. The efficiency of the meeting will be served because the other person will have the opportunity to agree with your interpretation or to correct it – in either case, things will be clearer. And the attentiveness and transparency which you demonstrate to the other person by sharing your hypothesis will be far more likely to enhance the relationship than the accuracy – or not – of your analysis.

Here are some examples of how you can apply the tools already encountered in previous chapters to dealing with the other person's unspoken communication.

Example 1: Understanding what's happening when you have no hypothesis

Imagine that whilst you're making a presentation, you've noticed that a key participant is sitting back in her chair with her hands clasped under chin and staring fixedly at the ceiling. You have no idea what's going on. Is this her way of showing that she's totally focused on what you're saying? Or is she just as totally distracted by something else? Or does her posture indicate something different entirely? In any case, you feel that in the context of your presentation something significant is happening and you want to know what it is. Then just say so!

> **You:** I may be prying too much . . . but I want to know what the significance for my presentation is of your intense focus on the ceiling right now. (*ME*)

Or

> **You:** In the context of my presentation, how am I to interpret the fact that you're staring intently at the ceiling with your hands clasped? (*ME*)

Example 2: Testing your hypothesis when you have one

Imagine that in a similar meeting, the key participant is instead sitting back in his chair with his arms folded and with what looks like a grimace on his face. Aha! You've read about this one in a body language textbook! It looks to you (perhaps) as if the participant is not being very receptive to your presentation. Rather than assuming this hypothesis to be correct and then, without acknowledging what you're doing, suddenly speeding up your delivery and trying to make more eye contact in the hope of engaging the participant more, just be open about what's happening in your head:

> **You:** Based on your posture and your expression right now, I'm thinking that so far I'm not blowing your socks off with my presentation.
>
> **Participant:** *No, the presentation's very interesting but can you please do something about the air-conditioning because it's like the South Pole in here!*
>
> **You:** I'm relieved to hear that about the presentation – and I'll get the thermostat turned up.

Or perhaps your hypothesis is correct after all:

> **You:** Based on your posture and your expression right now, I'm thinking that so far I'm not blowing your socks off with my presentation.
>
> **Participant:** *Well . . . I admit I AM very concerned about just how feasible your proposals are.*
>
> **You:** In that case, I want to pause and show you the detailed numbers before we go any further. (*ME*)

Or perhaps:

> **You:** What do I need to do to reassure you on that point? (*US*)

In either case, whether your interpretation of the other person's body language was right or wrong, the productivity of the meeting has been served. And the fact that you have been open about what's happening in your head, right or wrong, can only have a positive impact on the relationship as well. This is what I mean when I say that what you do with your interpretation is more important than its accuracy. Misinterpreting the other person's body language but being open about the hypothesis you've formed will better serve the relationship than interpreting their body language correctly but remaining covert about what you're doing.

Example 3: Dealing with inconsistency between what you hear and what you see

In the examples above, your response was based on the participants' unspoken communication alone. Sometimes it may be based on a perceived inconsistency between the unspoken and the spoken. Imagine that at the end of your presentation, you ask the participant what he thought of it and he responds by saying: *"It was fascinating"*. But perhaps the expression on his face and his tone of voice suggest to you that he actually means the exact opposite.

> **Participant:** *It was fascinating.*
>
> **You:** I wish I could take that at face value . . . but from your expression and your tone of voice I tell myself that I'm on the receiving end of some irony here. (*ME*)
>
> **Participant:** *Well, you did spend a lot of time on what I think are some very minor details.*
>
> **You:** What can I do to retrieve the situation? (*US*)

Example 4: Unspoken gestures

I was once presenting the Interactifs Discipline to a prospective client in a law firm who had invited me in to meet a small number of decision-makers and influencers. I mentioned in my introduction to the meeting that there are many training programmes in the general area of dealing more effectively with others which adopt a very psychological approach. The moment I mentioned the word "psychological", two people at the corner of the table exchanged a glance. The glance took about a nano-second but it was clear to me that something UNSAID was going on in the room which might possibly have a bearing on the success – or not – of my meeting. I decided that it would help me in the management of my meeting – and in the pursuit of my objectives – if I could get the unsaid said.

If the reason for this rapid exchange of glances had been a complete mystery to me and I had had no hypothesis as to what had triggered it, I could have used "HIM/HER" to identify the catalyst:

> **Me:** It seemed to me that when I mentioned the word "psychological", you two gentlemen exchanged a quick glance. And I'm wondering how I should interpret that glance.

As it happened, I did have a hypothesis about what had caused the glance to be exchanged, so instead I chose "ME", and this is how the conversation went:

> **Me:** I couldn't help noticing just now that when I mentioned the word "psychological", you two gentlemen exchanged a glance. And I'm telling myself that perhaps I have in the room people with some background in psychology.
>
> **Prospect:** *Yes, actually my colleague here is a clinical psychotherapist.*
>
> **Me (turning to the clinical psychotherapist):** In that context, how do you feel about what I've just been saying about training courses that take a very psychological approach?
>
> **Clinical psychotherapist:** *Well, I share your concerns because I studied for six years and I find it rather insulting when people suggest that useful psychology can be taught in two days!*

This was helpful information for me to have in the context of the meeting and of my objective; and it was using the tools to get the unsaid said, to find the meaning of an unspoken gesture, which allowed me to uncover the information.

2. Dealing with Your Own Non-verbal Communication

We all communicate unconsciously through our gestures, postures and expressions; and we all make at least some effort to do so consciously as well. Here's my point of view on your own unconscious and conscious non-verbal communication.

Unconscious Non-verbal Communication

However much you may wish consciously to control your non-verbal communication, you will never be able to control all of it. You can't switch off your unconscious mind. (This is one reason why body language experts look for several simultaneous body language signals: they know that the owner of the body in question may be faking some of the signals but can't fake all of them.)

Your body will therefore always unconsciously be providing indications about what you're really thinking or feeling. Most of the people you speak to won't be body language experts, so many of those indications will go unobserved or at least unanalysed. But you'll usually be speaking to people with significant experience of life as a human being – and therefore in possession of innate interpretation skills. Even if the other person doesn't know what every signal means, he or she will be pretty good at instinctively picking up different kinds of inconsistency, any of which will have negative consequences for the generation of confidence and trust. There may be inconsistency between your conscious and your unconscious non-verbal signals; there may be inconsistency between the words coming out of your mouth and your unconscious body language; or there may be inconsistency in the fact that your body seems to be saying something but your mouth remains closed.

If, as I have encouraged (and, I hope, enabled) you to do throughout the book, you ensure that (i) when you think or feel something, then you also say it, and (ii) you only say things which you really do think or feel, then you won't need to worry about your unconscious body language. It will – with no effort on your part – reflect what's happening in your head and therefore be entirely consistent with what you're saying. The generation of trust and confidence will be assured.

Conscious Non-verbal Communication

Conscious non-verbal communication seems to be used in two distinct ways. We all consciously use non-verbal gestures to communicate with the other person's *conscious* mind. But some of us, making more perverse use of what the scientific study of body language has uncovered for us, also try consciously to use non-verbal signals to communicate subliminally with the other person's *unconscious* mind.

I have talked above about the risks for the relationship of consciously using non-verbal communication to convey something different from what we're really thinking or feeling: our unconscious (and inconsistent) body language will give us away. But more often, we also consciously use gestures, postures or expressions to convey what we ARE thinking or feeling, as a substitute for actually saying it. Here too, we're running risks – or, at the very least, missing opportunities.

The unspoken can be immensely eloquent, but it is also a potentially inefficient medium for passing messages. The message may not be received, it may only be partially received, or it may get garbled in transmission and misunderstood. If your unspoken message is negative (a frown, an audible sigh, a look of disapproval, a rolling of the eyes) then, as already explained in Chapter 6, there are two possibilities. Either your message WILL be understood, but you will be seen as cowardly or downright disagreeable for having conveyed it implicitly rather than explicitly; or it will NOT be understood (or not correctly) in which case your communication has been either inefficient or ineffective or both.

When your unspoken message is positive – a warm smile, a wink, a touch of the arm, a thumbs-up – there's no jeopardy for the relationship. But perhaps you're just not taking full advantage of the opportunity to ENHANCE the relationship. If you're pleased to see a colleague, a warm smile will convey that perfectly adequately – but a warm smile accompanied by the words *"I'm really pleased to see you"* will have more impact. Moving your head ever closer to your dance partner's (see Chapter 8!) until your mouths are almost touching will certainly adequately convey that you're ready for a kiss – but if you accompany your gesture with the words *"I really want to kiss you"*, you will again make a much more positive impact!

Things get far darker when you consciously set out to use your body language to convey subliminal messages to the other person's unconscious mind. Now you will definitely be placing the relationship in jeopardy. I invite you to consider the importance for relationships of the principle of "do as you would be done by." Don't do stuff to other people you wouldn't want them to do to you.

As an example, I recently came across a "technique" in a book which recommended taking up more room in a meeting by spreading your papers and other effects across a large proportion of the table to convey an increased sense of your scale and importance. Would you want someone else to try to work on your unconscious mind and convey to you how important they are by placing their pencils right under your nose? I thought not. And beware: the book which recommended this was a best-seller in the genre, so the other people in your meeting may have read it too; and if you try this "technique" on them, they'll know exactly what you're doing and will probably view you as being much less consequential than you are rather than more so. (In contrast, I'm confident that no one you deal with who has also read THIS book will mistrust you for following its advice, because of the emphasis it places on transparency.)

Chapter Summary

- Non-verbal communication plays a hugely important role in human interaction; but the science of body language is sometimes perverted in business and used in ways which compromise the quality of the exchange.

- What you do with your interpretations of the other person's non-verbal signals is more important for the productivity of the meeting and the enhancement of the relationship than the accuracy of those interpretations. Share them openly with the other person and ask him or her to react.

- The tools you have previously encountered in the book for bringing clarity, comprehension and completeness to spoken communication can be used in the same ways and to the same ends with unspoken communication.

12

"What do you think?"

What you will have acquired by the end of the chapter:

An understanding of how to apply the principle of quality control, so important in production processes, to meetings and conversations.

In Chapter 4, I used an analogy comparing a meeting to a production process, a process initiated to manufacture a concrete finished product whose parameters are defined and agreed at the beginning of the process. I shall return to this analogy by insisting on the application in meetings of an element essential to any production process: quality control.

Quality control on a production line is obviously applied *at the end* of the line to check that the product has indeed been manufactured to the required specifications. Just as importantly, quality control is applied *throughout* the production process to ensure that the product is being manufactured as required – and to pick up and address any quality problems as they occur so that they don't have an impact on the final product.

The same principles should be applied to meetings, with measurements taken during the meeting, to ensure that the defined and agreed outcome *is being* produced; and at the end of the meeting, to ensure it *has been* produced.

Up until this point, the analogy is robust; but humans are plainly more complex than machines. Production lines just produce. People need to want to produce. Unless you have the other person under some form of constraint (which is rarely possible and always undesirable), they will only agree to do things for you, or with you, if you have inspired them with adequate quantities of respect, trust or affection. The measurement of the presence – or absence – of these elements is an additional form of quality assurance necessary, in appropriate doses, in human interactions.

Quality control in relationships, and in the meetings and conversations which are the building blocks of those relationships, entails finding out what the other person thinks of:

- My idea/argument/objective/response
- The meeting/the conversation/the work done together
- Me

"What Do You Think of What I Just Said?"

I started to air the principle of quality control during a meeting in Chapter 10, when I suggested that you should expose your arguments/thoughts/ideas one at a time – and then get the other person's reaction to each of them. Effective quality control requires measuring the impact of each item, as soon as you have exposed it, on your progress towards achieving the outcome you want at the end of the meeting.

For example, when I'm in a meeting with a prospective client and they enquire about the price we charge for our training programme, then after I've answered the question I always make sure that I ask what they think of my answer. The response immediately gives me a clear idea of the role price will play in the sale.

We may be more evolved than goldfish, but the short-term memory capacity of an average human brain is still limited. If you want to find out what the other person thinks of what you've just said, then you need to ask him or her immediately after you've said it. There's no point in making a five-minute speech full of powerful, cogent and erudite arguments and then asking the other person what he or she thinks of them. By then, he or she will have forgotten at least the first four minutes of the speech. Your sparkling arguments will have produced absolutely nothing. In a meeting or a conversation, try therefore to express yourself *one idea at a time; and then ask the other person what they think of what you've just said.* Not only will you give your arguments more chance to produce something, you will make considerably more impact:

- *Less is more.* The less you speak in a meeting, the more concise your phrases, the more impact you will have. The question "What do you think?" is a marvellously simple cure for talking too much. (You can use any similar formula you choose: "How do you react to that?" "What's your impression of what I've just said?", "How do you feel about that?" – or you can just raise your eyebrows or spread your palms to indicate to the other person that it's his or her turn to speak.)

- *Arguments are diminished in company.* Contrary to what most people seem to believe, piling up 10 arguments one on top of the other will diminish your impact, not increase it. If you find yourself embarking on a long speech punctuated by ". . . and another thing . . .", ". . . and have you thought about . . .", ". . . oh and by the way . . .", you should ask yourself whether you may not be starting to sound desperate. Arguments on their own are lean and hungry, like the wolf. In company, they're more likely to resemble sheep.

Let's go back to a meeting example I used in Chapter 3, the manager who needs to deal with a subordinate who is consistently late. It's entirely possible that early in the conversation, the subordinate may ask: "But surely getting the job done, which I do, is what counts. Why is time-keeping so important?"

The temptation when faced with such a question is to answer by piling up arguments one on top of another until you feel you've built such a strong case that no one can resist:

Subordinate: Why is time-keeping so important?

Manager: *Well, it's absolutely vital for the smooth running of the team. If YOU'RE late, everyone else will think they can be late. That's exactly what's starting to happen. It's very selfish and inconsiderate of you. How do you expect me to run meetings efficiently if people think they can turn up whenever they like? Plus you made me look like an idiot yesterday when my boss came along and no one was in the room yet. In fact she gave me a rollicking after the meeting which was entirely your fault. And another thing is that . . . (and so on for another five minutes).*

Your arguments will have more impact, and you will be able to measure very precisely what impact they have had, if you use them one at a time and invite the other person to respond to them:

Subordinate: Why is time-keeping so important?

Manager: *Well, it's important <u>to me</u> firstly because I feel I have a responsibility to the whole team to ensure their time is used efficiently and if I tolerate people coming late to meetings I don't feel I'm assuming that responsibility properly. How do you react to that?*

Subordinate: I suppose you have a point.

Manager: *So what do we do?*

Subordinate: I guess I'll have to make more of an effort in the future.

Manager: *I think we're moving in the right direction. But I need more than that . . .*

In this example, the argument given by the manager may or may not cut any ice with the subordinate, but at least the manager will know very precisely what her argument has produced. If it produces something positive (as it did in the dialogue I invented), then she won't need to get any other arguments out, saving both herself and the subordinate a lot of time. If the argument produces nothing, or

167

resistance, then she will need to find another argument but she will again use it singly and measure its impact: one argument at a time → *What do you think?*

The Interactifs Discipline can help the manager in lots of ways, beyond the ideas I suggested in Chapter 3 for opening the meeting. If she gets out, say, three arguments and they're all shot down in flames, she'd be legitimate in saying: "I get the impression that whatever arguments I come out with, and independent of any merit they may or may not have, they're going to be resisted. What do you say to that?" (ME)

Before getting out any of her arguments, she might choose to ensure she's not wasting time by asking: "Before I explain my reasons, I just need you to reassure me that I have a real chance of seeing you change, as long as you find that those reasons stand up." (US)

Before getting her arguments out, she might choose to enlist her subordinate's help in focusing only on arguments which stand any chance of producing something: "Well, there are lots of reasons why time-keeping is important for me. But before I go through them all, tell me, what are the kinds of areas which I need to focus on for me to have a hope of you changing your behaviour?"

Note also that in the two examples I gave above of a response to the question "Why is time-keeping so important?", the first example not only contained arguments which were piled up one on top of another, but those arguments also all focused on "it" and "you". The manager will be more legitimate and less likely to encounter resistance if she uses arguments focused on "I" as she did in the second example.

"What do you think?" or its equivalent will also allow you to ensure the arguments you deploy in support of a sale are give their best chance of success. An effective and credible sales argument is composed of three elements: (i) a feature; (ii) a benefit; (iii) "What do you think about that?" Any position regarding the product or service, any subjective, laudatory adjectives, any paeans of praise should come from the CUSTOMER and not from the salesperson; and "What do you think?" will help this to be the case.

A car salesman who says: "This one is incredibly economical. Sips petrol. Very abstemious. You'll hardly ever have to fill it up. Does 50 to the gallon in the urban cycle" is just being a salesman. He would say that, wouldn't he? A car salesman who says: "This model has a new engine which uses XYZ technology. The result is that on average it does 50mpg in the urban cycle. How do you find that?" is giving himself a chance that it will be the CUSTOMER who says "That's incredibly economical! Very abstemious! I'll hardly ever have to fill it up!" Praise from a customer will always be more productive in terms of the sale than praise from the salesman.

"What Did You Think of the Meeting?"

You can be certain that when you hold a meeting, the other person (or people) will leave the room with an opinion on how the meeting went. It would be very surprising if you didn't wonder what that opinion is. Why not just ask? Asking "What did you think of the meeting today?" (or "How was the meeting for you today" or "What did you think of the way that I handled the meeting today?" but NOT "Was everything OK?") will:

- Demonstrate your openness to hearing the other person's opinion, your courage and humility in subjecting yourself to the other person's judgement. This, regardless of the answer they provide (and of how explicit it is), is in itself likely to make a positive impression.

- Give you a chance of finding out what the other person's opinion actually is, with significant potential benefits for the way you run meetings with them in the future and for identifying and addressing any issues arising from THIS meeting.

How might this work in practice?

> **You:** Before the meeting closes, I want to know how you think it went today?
>
> **Client:** *I thought it was a very productive meeting. You were very clear about the goals right from the start and as a result we got a lot done in relatively short time. I was very happy with the meeting.*
>
> **You:** Great. That's my view as well. I'm absolutely delighted to hear you say that. (*ME*) And based on our feedback, I'll feel authorized to run our meetings like this in the future. (*ME*)

It won't always be that rosy:

> **You:** Before the meeting closes, I want to know how you think it went today?
>
> **Client:** *I thought it was pretty shambolic.*
>
> **You (Option 1 – you're surprised):** You've taken me by surprise there as I was feeling that it had gone fine.
> **You (Option 2 – you're not surprised):** I sadly share that view.
>
> **You: (Options 1 and 2):** How should I, in your view, run our meetings in the future so that you're 100 per cent happy with the way they go?
>
> **Client:** *Less PowerPoint, more dialogue, sharper focus on the objectives, more discipline in terms of time-keeping.*
>
> **You:** OK, will do.

(Now you've got the specifications for a successful meeting next time. Contrast this with the outcome if instead you'd asked: "Why did you think it was shambolic?")

The most likely response, particularly when you START asking this question of your clients and colleagues, may be more nuanced than either of the extremes above:

> **You:** Well, I'm disappointed we didn't achieve the objectives today but I'm confident we've now done the groundwork necessary to get them achieved when we meet next week. Beyond that, I want to ask you, how in general do you think I handled the meeting today?
>
> **Client:** It was fine.
>
> **You:** What exactly do you mean by "fine"? I need you to be more precise. (*HIM/HER*)

Or perhaps instead:

> **You:** The word "fine" makes me think that there's room for improvement next time. How do you feel about that? (*ME*)

Or:

> **You:** What can I do in the way I run meetings in the future so that instead of telling me it was "fine", you feel able to tell me it was "fantastic"? (*US*)

If you're uncomfortable about asking "What did you think of the meeting?" or unsure about how the other person will react, then you should just say that:

> **You:** I've got a question I want to ask which I'm not sure how you'll react to, but which I believe is an important one. What did you think about how the meeting went today?

Or even

> **You:** I've just been reading a book which suggested systematically asking a specific quality control question at the end of meetings and I thought I'd give it a try today to see what

happens. Here it is: "How did you feel the meeting went this morning?"

Once you've got your answer, you can also ask:

You: And what did you think about me asking this kind of question at the end of the meeting?

Note that doing a recap of what was agreed at the end of the meeting (as is often the case) is NOT the same as asking the other person how the meeting went. Achieving the meeting goals and enhancing the relationship between the parties are not always mutually inclusive.

"What Do You Think of ME?"

This is clearly a delicate question to ask. It is likely to be used once only with a given person, when the need arises. The following are circumstances where the question is legitimate and where the information it provides will be important for you:

- *When there seems to be a problem in your working relationship with someone*

  Perhaps you have a difficult relationship with a colleague: every time you meet, you end up shouting at each other, the work you ask for never gets done, your emails don't get answered. You may be starting to wonder if the person has a problem with you personally and you need to find out, probably by initiating a meeting specifically to address the issue, with an objective such as: "I want us to agree on how we can work together in the future in a way we're both much happier with". (This is similar to the objective I suggested in the example in Chapter 5, when the difficult working relationship was with your boss.)

172

It may be that your colleague is going through a difficult time in his personal life and has decided to take his unhappiness out on you – and on everyone else. He doesn't specifically dislike or distrust you any more than he does anyone else. Or it may be that he does specifically dislike or distrust you. You need to know what's going on and you need to work on what you can do to change the situation.

In this context, "What do you think of me?" will be an indispensable question to ask. The question will almost certainly be unexpected, so it may help you to be comfortable asking it if you preface the question with an explanation of why you're asking it: "Look, I get the feeling that whenever we meet things go horribly wrong and I'm determined for us to find a way of sorting this out. In order for there to be any chance of that happening, I think it's important for me to know what you actually think of me".

- *When the impression left has an incidence on the rest of the relationship and the next steps*

Imagine you are pitching for a major project at Megacorp, a prospect you have had on your radar for a while. You have just made a presentation to the decision-maker and the impression you and your team have left on him will be a major factor in his decision to include you – or not – in the shortlist of consulted suppliers.

Rather than looking at each other in the lift and asking yourselves what impression you left, how about asking the decision-maker in person before leaving the meeting? "What do you think of me and my team after today's meeting?" Or perhaps: "Given that relationships are obviously crucial when it comes to choosing partners, I'd like to know what impression I and my colleagues have left on you today?" Again, regardless of the other person's answer (because the prospect may find the question surprising and not be completely frank in their answer), half of the job is done just by asking the question.

- *When aspersions seem to be being made about the entire professional category to which you belong*

Perhaps the person opposite you has just implicitly damned you by including you in a category he or she apparently despises: "You bankers, you're all the same, only interested in what you can gouge out of a customer" or "Car salesmen! I ask you! You're all as bent as each other!" or "Insurance companies – you're all very happy to take our money but not so happy when it comes to giving back what we've paid for!"

Implicit in these remarks is the opinion that YOU want to gouge money out of clients or that YOU are bent or that YOU don't like paying out on policies. You will be better able to deal with the situation if you invite the person opposite to be explicit and to take a clear position regarding YOU. For example:

Customer: You bankers, you're all the same, only interested in what you can gouge out of customers!
You: And what do you think of ME?

The answer to that question will give you a much clearer idea of what's really going on. There's a difference between a customer who answers "You? You're the biggest crook of the lot!" and one who answers "Well, I've got nothing against you personally".

The question will be just as valuable if a customer complements your predecessor: "Emily did such a great job!".

- *When you just need to know!*

Philippe tells me that he was once asked for advice by a client worried about his (grown-up) daughter. The client felt that she was highly capable, greatly respected by her colleagues at work

– but very short of self-confidence. Philippe suggested that she just ask thirty or so of her colleagues what they thought of her. The answers she got boosted her self-confidence immeasurably.

Note: although many companies use customer satisfaction surveys as a quality control measure, these should be seen as complementary to asking someone face to face what they think rather than as a substitute for doing so. Surveys can generate lots of useful data; asking the question face to face will generate respect and esteem.

"Yes" or "No" Is Not Feedback

Asking for feedback but only giving the other person a binary option ("Did you like the chicken?" "Was the presentation OK?" "Does my bum look big in this?") will neither give you useful information nor make a positive impression on the other person. Because of the problems people have in being direct, the other person will probably, in response to the above questions, choose the most comfortable option: "Yes I did", "Yes it was" or "No it doesn't". Indeed questions like those above are not really questions – they are suggested answers and give the impression that you're not really interested in the other person's opinion, just in hearing what you want to hear. Don't be surprised if you get the answer you suggested. You still won't really know what the other person thinks; and the other person won't go away thinking his or her opinion is important to you.

Imagine you're a restaurateur with a new restaurant and you decide to do quality control with your customers at the end of each meal. If you walk from table to table and ask your clients: "Were you happy with the meal, sir?", or "Was everything OK?" (which is what you'll hear from most restaurant owners seeking feedback) then unless the meal was a complete catastrophe, they won't be comfortable saying "No".

So instead they'll say "Yes", the only other choice you gave them, the answer you suggested you wanted to hear. You haven't learnt anything useful and actionable; and you haven't demonstrated to your customers that their opinion matters to you. If there are minor problems with the meals you're not going to identify them and be able to do anything about them. "What did you think of the meal?" will get you a much richer, more nuanced response: "I thought the soup was sublime, the fish out of this world, but, if I could make one small comment, I thought the 'crème brûlée' was a little too 'brûlée' for my taste". Now you've got useful information that will help you to improve. You've also asked a question which is much more likely to enhance the image of your restaurant with its customers.

"What Do You Think of the Book?"

As you're almost at the end of the book and we're talking about feedback, I feel that this is an appropriate place to ask you to go to **www.talk-lean.com/feedback** to tell me what you thought of it. There will be no yes/no questions!

Chapter Summary

- Quality control is essential in a meeting to check the impact of thoughts/arguments/ideas/answers as they are delivered; and to check what the meeting has produced at the level of results and relationships.

- Quality control in a meeting takes three forms: (i) what do you think of what I just said (after each thought, idea, argument); (ii) what did you think of the meeting (after each event); and (iii) what do you think of me (only once).

THE INTERACTIFS DISCIPLINE: SCHEMATICS

1. I prepare	2. I start
(i) I choose my meeting objective (ii) What I did to prepare the meeting (iii) My state of mind	(i) My state of mind (ii) What I did to prepare the meeting (iii) My objective What do you think?

3. I listen

(i) I listen to him/her. I take notes, I write down what he/she says, in his/her order, in his/her words (at least the first words)

(ii) I listen to myself, to the impact those words have had on me

4. I respond

HIM/HER	ME	US
"What do you mean by ...?"	"Hearing you say..., I tell myself ... What do you think?"	"What do I need to do so that you...?"
"What leads/led you to do/say...?"	"I want (I'd like)... What do you think?"	"If I..., what will you do?"
"Tell me more about..."	"I need...What do you think?"	"What do we do?"

5. I measure

(i) "What do you think of what I've just said?" (After each idea/thought/argument/response)

(ii) "What did you think of the meeting/the way I handled the meeting/what the meeting produced?" (After each event)

(iii) "What do you think of me?" (Once only)

178

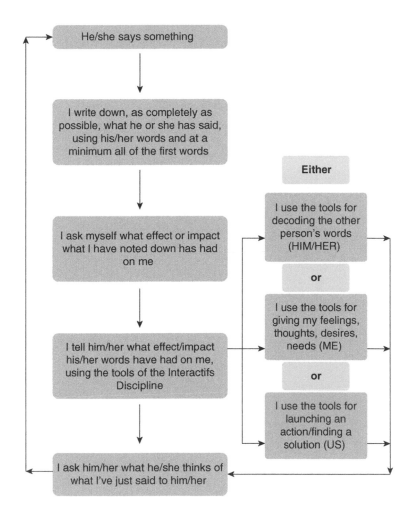

INTERACTIFS TRAINING PROGRAMMES

As these single-page schematics confirm, the "Interactifs Discipline" is conceptually simple and based entirely on the application of sound, practical common sense. However, using the approach often requires the replacement of life-long reflexes with new ones. Whether your field is sport, music, or meetings, the acquisition of new reflexes demands practice and repetition. This is reflected in the structure of our training programmes: 80% of the content of our courses is devoted to intensive practice in the use of the Discipline in the context of the real-life business situations encountered by the course participants.

For further information on our in-house and open-enrolment programmes in 10 languages, please visit: **http://www.interactifs.co.uk/ programmes** or **www.talk-lean.com/programmes**

Feedback on the Interactifs Programme

"Why on different occasions and in different jobs have I had my teams trained in the Interactifs Discipline? . . . Quite simply because, every time, the impact on our business has been real and visible. For

example, I am convinced that when all seemed lost in a particular moment of intense and difficult negotiation with one of our biggest international clients, it was the Interactifs tools which allowed us to turn the situation around and renew the client relationship against all the odds."
Robert Guillet, Global Vice-President Customer Development, Unilever Food Solutions

"I have been introduced to an exceptional approach for increasing my effectiveness and I will start getting the benefits from it in all my meetings both business and personal right away. Spend two days but gain one hundred at least."
Carol Fedida, Founder, Flower City Ltd

"I recently attended an 'Interactifs' seminar on 'Impact and Influence' with Alan and it was fantastic. Alan's delivery was insightful and tailored to each person requirements of the seminar. The way Alan ran the seminar has allowed me to transition what I learnt quickly into my role."
Andrew Parks, Deputy Programme Manager, Babcock International

"Alan's training is highly effective – focusing on simpler, more productive and effective meetings, his coaching strategies deliver immediate results."
Adrian Rafferty, Founder, Opus Lex Consulting

"I attended an 'Influence and Impact' seminar run by Alan. Superb communicator with great people skills delivering an innovative and fascinating training programme that should reap significant benefit to my business in time."
Andrew Mallinson, Director, Intelliprice

"I had the pleasure of attending one of Alan's 2-day communication courses – it blew my mind. Some very simple concepts – yet so incredibly effective! We got time to test and implement the approach, which I found extremely helpful. I still use his ideas today – they have made me much more effective and I have also learned to listen better as a result. Awesome!"

Rahima Valji, former Managing Director, iTravel UK

"I made the great decision to do Alan's 2-day course on dealing more productively with other people. It was a very inspiring and productive course and probably the best two days I have ever invested. Should be mandatory for all (smart) organizations. Great value and excellently taught."

Carl-Johan Collett, Development Manager (Affordable Housing Program), First Quantum Minerals Ltd

"I was delighted to be able to attend your course earlier this year and am very pleased to say that, of all the courses we have procured this year, Interactifs has had the biggest impact on how we work. Thanks!"

Mike Meredith, Director, 2020 Delivery

"I was blown away by how effective these communications tools are."

Laurence Miall d'Août, Director of TV, TalkTalk

"Coming from an organization that takes pride in developing leadership for testing circumstances in unpredictable environments, I was intrigued to discover the approach employed by Alan and Interactifs to attain greater impact and influence. The course was fascinating and beneficial, and espoused effective ways of dealing with others that I utilize today. Alan proved to be an excellent trainer, making the process highly interactive, informative and enjoyable. I am very happy to recommend Alan and the Interactifs experience."

Charlie Waggett, Lieutenant-Colonel, HM Forces

"I participated in an Interactifs seminar a couple of years ago. One of the 'challenging situations' that I chose to practice during the seminar was a series of meetings which we were about to start with a prominent UK-wide chain of coffee shops – an important prospective customer for us. The seminar helped me to clarify and structure my objectives in advance of each meeting and to participate in the meetings in a way that allowed the client's concerns about trading with a new, relatively small supplier to be addressed early and openly. The clarity of the method helped me to focus naturally on the needs of the other party and to demonstrate a real willingness to listen. The emphasis on always asking questions means that the effect builds as meetings and the overall relationship progress. The meetings concluded with a first order – and the coffee-shop chain is now one of our biggest customers."

Sir Parry Hughes-Morgan, Bt, Managing Director, The Handmade Cake Company

"Alan's workshop was excellent. The people present, comprising of mainly senior executives, found the course content to be highly relevant and a revelation on how to communicate more effectively with others; in particular, how to best position yourself to get positive results from a discussion. I would recommend this course to anyone who wants to be more effective in pitches, business meetings and the like."

Claire Leach, Director of Development, FareShare (Melbourne)

"I can't thank you enough for the seminar last week. It was a thoughtful and stimulating couple of days resulting in lasting learning. I already can sense that I approach meetings differently. I will wholeheartedly give you 100 recommendations – it is a course well worth doing in business – at any stage of one's career."

Memoria Lewis, Membership Director, Institute and Faculty of Actuaries

"I attended the 'Impact and Influence' programme which was led by Alan recently and it proved to be two very well-invested days. I am cynical about workshop sessions and training but Alan brought with him a life of very relevant experience combined with a quick and creative attitude in working with the participants – a class act (as they say). The content of the programme itself is straight-forward and pragmatic: something of immense value which can be applied at once."

Dominic Rowsell, EMEIA Pursuits Leader, Ernst & Young LLP

ABOUT THE AUTHOR

Alan H. Palmer was born in London. He was educated at Oxford and INSEAD and has spent most of his career working for international advertising agency groups in London and Paris. He first came across Interactifs in 2004 and was instantly persuaded of the effectiveness of the company's approach, its applicability across national boundaries – and its capacity, in a modest way, to contribute to the sum total of human happiness.

He subsequently joined the company both to deliver training programmes and to help develop Interactifs' business around the world, and in particular in the UK. He regularly runs seminars in Britain but has also done so in France, the Netherlands, Poland, Spain, Switzerland, Turkey, the United Arab Emirates and China. Alan is married with three children and lives near Fontainebleau, but divides his professional time between London and Paris. He can be contacted at: **alan.palmer@interactifs.com**.

The Originator of the Interactifs Discipline

Philippe de Lapoyade was born in Sainte Foy la Grande in southwest France. He spent the early part of his career working in sales and management roles for blue-chip consumer goods companies and found himself responsible for spending large sums of his employers' money on sales and management training. There were aspects of these programmes which he liked – but many that he did not, most notably the emphasis on unacknowledged manipulation and simplistic psychology.

Being of an intellectually curious nature, he set himself the task of developing something which was simpler, more effective and capable of being used with a clearer conscience. What he developed is described in this book. He established a company, Interactifs (**www.interactifs.com**), in 1989 to offer his approach to companies and organizations and today has some 80 trainers working with him delivering the training to financial institutions, automotive companies, consultancy firms, service industries, manufacturers and within business schools. The company delivers training in 10 different languages (English, French, German, Italian, Spanish, Dutch, Portuguese, Czech, Romanian and Turkish) and has worked in over 20 countries. Philippe is married with five children and divides his time between Paris and Sainte Foy la Grande. He can be contacted at: **philippe.de.lapoyade@interactifs.com**.

Contributor

Clément Toulemonde was born in Paris but spent his childhood in New Zealand, South Korea, Morocco and Australia. He took his Bachelor's and Master's degrees at the University of New South Wales in Sydney.

After graduating, he worked as a management consultant, initially in Australia and then in France. It was as a manager in Paris that he first came across Interactifs when he participated in a seminar – and within a short period of time he had decided to join the company himself. Today he is a partner at Interactifs and responsible for the Group's development in the English-speaking world and throughout Asia-Pacific. He regularly runs seminars (as do all of Interactifs' management) in French and English for many of the company's major clients. Clément lives with his wife and twins just outside Paris. He can be contacted at: **clement.toulemonde@interactifs.com**.

INDEX

INDEX

INDEX

INDEX

production process 40, 60, 62,
163, 164
productivity 11, 25, 30, 36, 39, 41,
42, 56, 64, 73, 75, 77, 78, 79, 83,
85, 97, 117, 119, 123, 135, 139,
155, 161
professional 6, 10, 43, 174, 185
promise 11, 33, 34, 50, 53, 62. 63,
113, 114
prospect 4, 26, 29, 43, 44, 45, 46,
47, 65, 78, 123, 144, 146, 157,
173
prospective 7, 16, 45, 47, 123, 156,
165, 183
psychological 16, 17, 156, 157
psychology 17, 60, 157, 186
punctuality 34, 35, 70, 144

quality assurance 165
quality control 163, 164, 165, 171,
175, 176

raise 10, 27, 35, 36, 59, 70, 93,
104, 144, 166, 169
raw material 91, 93, 94, 97
reason 6, 8, 12, 20, 26, 30, 32, 33,
40, 43, 51, 52, 79, 86, 90, 102,
115, 120, 123, 130, 137, 139,
142, 157, 158, 168
reception 113, 114
receptive 6, 7, 10, 11, 28, 34, 41,
57, 59, 70, 76, 145, 154
reformulation 124, 125, 133
relationship 6, 9, 11–13, 18,
20–21, 31–32, 36–37, 40, 43–44,
46–47, 52–53, 56, 58–60, 64,
76–77, 79, 81, 103, 123
respect 6, 8, 10, 16, 19, 21, 28, 34,
35, 36, 37, 69, 128, 133, 165, 175
respectful 6, 7, 8, 20, 28, 29, 30,
66, 76, 82, 138
responding 52, 55, 89, 99, 101,
102, 103, 104, 105, 107, 109,

111, 113, 115, 116, 117, 119,
135, 139
responsibility 30, 167
result 6, 8–9, 11–12, 14, 20–21,
28, 37, 40, 44–46, 50, 56, 59,
65–66, 77, 80–82, 93, 95, 97,
101, 103, 104, 107
retail client 26, 32, 51, 52
rhetorical question 81
rigorous listening 90, 97

sale 5, 10, 13, 27, 29, 59, 89, 90,
92, 102, 103, 107, 125, 139, 168,
169, 186
salesman 10, 27, 35, 36, 43, 59,
82, 125, 126, 131, 169
scenario 7, 27, 65
script 30, 36, 67
seductive 7, 10, 126, 131, 132
self-assurance 80
self-confidence 175
selling 6, 43
seminar 43, 88, 112, 129, 133,
182, 183, 184, 185, 187
September 11th 89
short-term 13, 165
simple 9, 10, 12, 17, 21, 57, 58,
63, 70, 82, 88, 93, 104, 131, 136,
139, 166, 180, 182, 186
sincere 8, 66
social lubricant 66
solutions 36, 37, 95, 115, 181
solving problems 12, 136
speaking style 37, 68
spoken language 67, 69
square the circle 7
state of mind 60, 65, 66, 67, 68,
69, 70
straight to the point 20, 23, 27,
28, 37, 64, 66, 76, 100, 128
straight-away 25, 27, 29, 31, 33,
35, 37, 41, 54
straight-forward 184

Lightning Source UK Ltd.
Milton Keynes UK
UKOW06f2333310316

271270UK00005B/5/P

9 780857 084972